ALSO BY STACY McANULTY

SAVE THE PEOPLE! HALTING HUMAN EXTINCTION

WHERE ARE THE ALIENS?

THE SEARCH FOR LIFE BEYOND EARTH

STACY McANULTY

WITH ART BY NICOLE MILES

LB

LITTLE, BROWN AND COMPANY
New York Boston

Little, Brown and Company
Hachette Book Group
1290 Avenue of the Americas, New York, NY 10104
Visit us at LBYR.com

First Edition: September 2023

Little, Brown and Company is a division of Hachette Book Group, Inc.
The Little, Brown name and logo are trademarks of Hachette Book Group, Inc.

The publisher is not responsible for websites (or their content)
that are not owned by the publisher.

Little, Brown and Company books may be purchased in bulk for business, educational,
or promotional use. For information, please contact your local bookseller or the
Hachette Book Group Special Markets Department at special.markets@hbgusa.com.

Library of Congress Cataloging-in-Publication Data
Names: McAnulty, Stacy, author. | Miles, Nicole, illustrator.
Title: Where are the aliens? : the search for life beyond Earth /
Stacy McAnulty ; with art by Nicole Miles.
Description: First edition. | New York, NY : Little, Brown and Company, 2023. |
Includes bibliographical references and index. | Audience: Ages 10 and up | Summary:
"A deep-dive exploration into the many theories and discoveries surrounding the
possibility of extraterrestrial life beyond Earth." —Provided by publisher.
Identifiers: LCCN 2022058927 | ISBN 9780759553996
(hardcover) | ISBN 9780759554023 (ebook)
Subjects: LCSH: Life on other planets—Juvenile literature.
Classification: LCC QB54 .M525 2023 | DDC 576.8/39—dc23/eng20230424
LC record available at https://lccn.loc.gov/2022058927

ISBNs: 978-0-7595-5399-6 (hardcover), 978-0-7595-5402-3 (ebook)

Printed in the United States of America

LSC-C

Printing 2, 2023

FOR YOU, READER
(AND FUTURE EXTRATERRESTRIAL VISITORS)

CONTENTS

DEAR INQUISITIVE READER,

It seems you're on a quest to discover if we are alone in the universe. Maybe you want to know if there are aliens out there planning to invade our planet, or maybe you're interested in the hunt for ancient microbes on Mars. *Well, bad news.* While I appreciate you picking up my book, I need to be up front and honest: I don't have a definitive answer for you. *Sorry, Area 51 fans.* As of the printing of this edition, scientists haven't located life beyond Earth. But that shouldn't keep us from examining what we do know and what we hope to know in the near future. Let's contemplate what may or may not exist.

Before we get to alleged alien abductions and UFOs (unidentified flying objects), we need to ponder some brain teasers. Our journey will begin with the Fermi paradox, a famous question meant to spark debate or even some light yelling if there are strong opinions. Then we'll explore a bit of history, starting with the birth of the universe and focusing on the rise of life on our planet. From the big bang to pri-mordial soup, we'll puzzle over how it all happened. From there, we'll look at how past humans—like ancient Greeks and 1970s NASA scientists—have tried to answer our burn-ing question. No way are we the first generations to wonder about life among the stars. But maybe we have access to info that others did not.

Since *Homo sapiens* (meaning: us, our species) are the only animals required to take science classes, we will use our knowledge of the physical and natural world to our full advantage—though many of the answers we seek need further research. Luckily, scientists are actively looking for life both within our solar system *and* beyond. Some focus on teeny-tiny stuff like bacteria and even simple life-building chemicals, which means they don't just need telescopes—they need mi-croscopes. And SETI (search for extraterrestrial intelligence) scientists look and listen to deep space in hopes of discover-ing big-brained (or whatever the equivalent alien organ is) smarties who have developed communication methods.

Turns out *Homo sapiens* also have to take math classes. Good thing, because we're going to crunch some numbers. (Calculators are optional. I'll do most of the work.) We'll play around with the famous Drake equation and look at the odds of alien existence through the lens of probability. Like, if we had a giant bag with a trillion M&M'S, what's the chance we reach into that bag and pull out a purple one? (I hope you're asking yourself, "Do M&M'S come in purple?")

Finally, we'll look at a different kind of history—the history of alien contact with Earthlings. From the Roswell incident to UAPs (unidentified aerial phenomena) spotted by Navy pilots to alien abductions, what's going on with these reports? We'll dig for explanations.

Are you ready to hunt for little green men? Let's do this.

Sincerely,

Stacy

Your fearless alien-seeking guide

PS: Science is moving fast. I've tried to bring you the latest and greatest information, but discoveries are happening all. The. TIME! At the back of the book, I've included some trusted resources for keeping up-to-date.

PPS: A quick note on a style choice. Sometimes I will put an abbreviation first with its meaning in parentheses, like this: UFO (unidentified flying object). That's because the abbreviation is used more commonly. But sometimes I'll do the opposite—like this: Hubble Space Telescope (HST)—because the abbreviation isn't used as widely. My apologies if you find this annoying. There's a handy-dandy list of abbreviations at the end of the book.

CHAPTER 1

WHERE IS EVERYBODY?

MEET THE FERMI PARADOX

The universe has billions and billions of planets. Yet we know of only one that hosts any kind of life. *Yay for Earth! Yay for us!* But to be fair, astronomers have looked at only a fraction of the possibilities. (More like a fraction of a fraction.) Imagine going to the beach, scooping up a bucket of water, seeing no fish or other critters, and then declaring the ocean is void of life. That would be a ridiculous conclusion. But that's the situation scientists are in when searching for aliens. So far, nada, but the hunt has just begun.

This might lead us to believe that there are (maybe? probably? definitely?) extraterrestrials out there. We just haven't located them yet. If you agree, you're in the majority. According to a recent survey, 65 percent of American adults believe intelligent life (meaning: creatures who can understand and learn) exists on other planets. Let's call this optimistic group Life Beyond Earth–ers.

On the flip side, there's another group: those who believe

LIFE BEYOND EARTH-ER VS. ONLY EARTH-ER

There is no evidence proving life exists beyond Earth now or in the past. This could change at any moment with an amazing find on Mars (maybe microscopic organisms buried in the ice) or a communication from deep space (maybe a satellite picking up a text message from a planet in the Andromeda galaxy, 2.5 million light-years away). Until scientists prove otherwise, the question of "Does life exist beyond Earth?" is a matter of opinion—even if we use math to calculate odds. Whether you're a Life Beyond Earth-er or an Only Earth-er, you aren't technically wrong. You can flip back and forth as you learn more and think more about the topic. However, we must be careful that we don't apply this same mentality to other areas of science. For example, take the following facts.

- Earth is not flat. It is round.
- Our planet is approximately 4.54 billion years old.
- Human activity has caused climate change.
- Vaccines save lives.
- Dinosaurs roamed Earth for approximately 165 million years.
- Adding vinegar to baking soda will make a mess.

Each of these is a scientific consensus (meaning: the overwhelming majority of scientists in that field agree with the statement). It might be decades or centuries before we can add "Intelligent life has been found on..." to this list, and we'll never be able to definitely say, "Life exists only on Earth." There's just too much universe to explore.

life exists only here on our perfect planet. At this point, there is no evidence to the contrary. Let's call this team Only Earth-ers. Perhaps our world is so unique in its location and geological history that it's a one-in-a-billion-billion-billion scenario. Perhaps we really are that special! Only Earth–ers may argue that if there were *others*, we would have heard from them by now. *Right?* That is essentially the famous Fermi paradox.

WHERE IS EVERYBODY?

WHAT'S A FERMI?

First, you may be asking, "Who (or what) is Fermi?" Let me introduce Enrico Fermi, an Italian physicist born in 1901. Fermi was a smarty-pants who won scholarships and studied at notable European universities. After completing his education, he started working in the exciting new field of nuclear fission (meaning: the splitting of atoms, which results in a ton of energy). In 1938, he won the prestigious Nobel Prize in Physics. *Way to go, Enrico!* But the Nobel Prize wasn't just about bragging rights for Fermi. The prize money and fame allowed him and his wife, Laura, to get out of Italy, which had adopted some of Nazi Germany's antisemitic policies. Laura was Jewish, and it wasn't safe for them there. They immigrated to the United States. Fermi continued his work in nuclear science and eventually was part of the Manhattan Project, which created the first atomic bombs. Later, he would assist in developing even bigger bombs—the thermonuclear type, which uses fusion (meaning: the merging of atoms, creating tons and tons of energy). Even though a lot of his life's work revolved around bomb making, he did realize the dangers and wrote a letter of warning to President Truman.

Obviously, Enrico Fermi was an intelligent guy who knew about physics and math, but he was not an astronomer. And yet he may be best known for sparking a debate about aliens that's more than seventy years old.

A LUNCH TO REMEMBER

In 1950, Fermi was working at Los Alamos National Laboratory in New Mexico. One day, on the way to the cafeteria, Fermi and his physicist friends began discussing UFOs. The *New Yorker* magazine had run a cartoon about flying saucers. There'd also been a recent uptick in reported sightings, probably because of new aviation technology that put strange and unfamiliar objects in the skies (things like jets, rockets, and weather balloons). When the group sat down to lunch, the conversation changed to something else—no one seemed to recall what exactly—when suddenly Fermi asked, "Where is everyone?" The guys knew he wasn't talking about coworkers or any humans. He was asking, *Where are the aliens?* (Which is a good title for a book, *don't you think?*)

Not much came from the question immediately. No one had the answer. They all somewhat agreed that Earth likely resides in a rural-like area of the galaxy—not very crowded with life. Maybe other parts of the Milky Way were more like cities with lots of activity.

Apparently, the question stuck with Fermi beyond the cafeteria.

In the following days, he turned the question into a math problem. (This is something *we* will do several times in this book.) Fermi calculated the probability of other Earthlike planets in our galaxy, the probability of those planets having life, the probability of humanlike life, and how long they'd need to develop space travel. His rough calculations revealed that Earth should have been visited by extraterrestrials long ago and on numerous occasions.

Fermi died of cancer about four years after asking his famous question. He never wrote about extraterrestrials, UFOs, or outer space. (Remember, his expertise was nuclear physics.) But his lunch buddies recalled the conversation years later, and they say Fermi wasn't just talking about the existence of aliens. He was questioning the possibility of space travel. Basically, if intragalactic voyages were achievable, Earthlings should have noticed visitors by now.

FROM QUESTION TO PARADOX

Now you may be asking, "What is a paradox?" (Not to be confused with a "pair of docs," which is two physicians.) A paradox is a contradictory or absurd statement often meant to spur deep thought. A famous example is the liar's paradox, which works like this: Imagine we're chatting, and I say...

"My dog was in a commercial.

I hate licorice.

One time in Yellowstone, I hit a bison with my car.

Oh, and everything I'm saying is a lie."

The liar's paradox is really about that last line. If I am lying—like I said I was—that last statement would actually be a truth. Thus, I wouldn't be lying. How could I be both lying and not lying? On the flip side, if we assume that I'm not lying in that last line, then the statement would be a lie. Thus, I would be lying. Again, I can't be both.

In summary:

Statement	If...	Then...	Thus...
Everything I'm saying is a lie.	Lying	Statement is true	Not lying
Everything I'm saying is a lie.	Not lying	Statement is false	Lying

Another famous paradox is about the town barber. If the barber shaves only the men in town who do not shave themselves, who shaves the barber? *Well?* (Does your head hurt yet?)

For the record, none of my dogs have been in a commercial. I do hate licorice. I *almost* hit a bison in the summer of 2015. And I've lied at least once.

Enough about barbers and bison—back to focusing on Fermi. To those at the Los Alamos National Laboratory lunch table, Fermi wasn't being philosophical or overly deep. He simply asked a question on his mind after the group talked about UFOs and aliens. "Where is everyone?" It wasn't until the mid-1970s that this pondering would be called a paradox (though plenty of people argue it's not *truly* a paradox). If technologically advanced extraterrestrials were out there, we would have noticed them by now. They're not here, so they must not exist.

Obviously, we can see many flaws with the above statement. Lack of proof is not proof. Like looking in the bucket of ocean water.

IF THE SUN WERE THE SIZE OF A BASKETBALL...

The size of our galaxy is tough to comprehend. Sometimes, an analogy can help us picture it better.

	Actual Distance	**Imagine**
Sun Diameter	864,337 miles (1,391,016 km)	basketball
Earth Diameter	7,918 miles (12,743 km)	pea
Jupiter Diameter	86,881 miles (139,821 km)	baseball
To Nearest Star	4.2 light-years	About the distance from the USA to England
Milky Way Galaxy Diameter	100,000 light-years	Over 12,000 laps around Earth

Let's review our galaxy in terms of numbers and see why "Where is everybody?" is still quite a head-scratcher.

Some Numbers:

The Milky Way galaxy is about 100,000 light-years wide.

One light-year is the distance light travels in a year (about 5.88 trillion miles, or 9.46 trillion kilometers).

100,000 LIGHT-YEARS WIDE

The Milky Way is 13.6 billion years old.

Earth is about 4.54 billion years old.

Let's pretend that a planet named Luigi (the name of one of my dogs) was born in the early days of the Milky Way, like when our galaxy was just 4 billion years old. How long would it take for planet Luigi to develop intelligent life that would have the ability to visit Earth?

Imaginary Timeline:
- Milky Way: 4 billion years old
- Planet Luigi: 0 years old (a newborn planet)
- Planet Earth: about –5 billion years old (the best planet ever is worth the wait, IMHO)

Now let's give planet Luigi enough time to grow up and develop intelligent, science-loving creatures. We know that on Earth, this took about 4.54 billion years. Of course, we are smart but don't currently possess rocket ship technology capable of interstellar travel (meaning: journeying from one star system to another). So how long *will* it take us to develop interstellar rocket ship technology? Considering what humans have created in the past 100 years—nuclear weapons, satellites, lasers, Pop Its—in a billion years, we'll maybe/probably/definitely have the ability to travel to another star system. The closest we've gotten was when Voyagers 1 and 2 left our solar system, but still, they were nowhere close to entering another. (More in Chapter 4.)

To be on the safe side, let's give Luigians another billion years (for a total of 6.5 billion years) to develop really cool, fast, efficient rockets. These Luigian rockets can travel at 1 percent of the speed of light. *Zoom! Zoom!*

Imaginary Timeline (continued):

- Milky Way: 10.5 billion years old
- Planet Luigi: 6.5 billion years old (and Luigians are technological all-stars!)
- Planet Earth: 1.44 billion years old (life on our planet would have been microscopic at this time)

Now we've got an interstellar-voyaging species hopping around the Milky Way. Even traveling at just 1 percent of light speed, they'd cross the entire galaxy in a mere 10 million years.

That's because 1 percent of light speed is still mind-blowingly fast—like 6,706,000 miles (10,792,000 kilometers) per hour. The fastest Earthling-made spacecraft reached only about 365,000 miles (587,400 kilometers) per hour. Luigians are traveling over eighteen times faster than our fastest vehicle!

Believe the Math:

Milky Way Galaxy = 100,000 light-years wide

Luigians' Travel Speed = .01 light-years per year (1% in decimal form is .01)

Time to Zoom Across the Galaxy = Distance ÷ Speed

$$100,000 \div .01 = 10,000,000 \text{ years}$$

Even if the Luigians stopped at a million planets along the way and spent 1,000 years on each, building canals or pyramids or fueling stations, that's still just another billion years.

Imaginary Timeline (continued):

- Milky Way: 11.51 billion years old
- Planet Luigi: 7.51 billion years old
- Planet Earth: 2.45 billion years old (our world now has photosynthesis and oxygen)

It's possible the Luigians missed Earth on their first trek across the galaxy. Perhaps they thought our young solar system was boring. But that was about 2 billion years ago. Again, if they can travel at 1 percent of light speed, they could cross the galaxy 200 times in 2 billion years. Certainly they should have made contact with Earthlings by now!

And yet...*where is everybody?*

POSSIBLE ANSWERS TO THE FERMI QUESTION/ PARADOX

What could be the reasons for this "great silence"? Why isn't there *any* evidence of alien life?

- [ ] Choice A: We really are alone. It's just us. It's just Earth (at least for "smart" life). While that may be a bit disappointing to some, it's certainly a possibility. But unlike a search for Bigfoot or the Loch Ness monster, there are seemingly infinite places for aliens to hide. We're talking billions of planets in our galaxy and trillions of planets in the universe. And yet vastness alone does not mean something is out there. This is the answer Only Earth–ers would select. It's like asking, "Why didn't the phone ring?" The obvious (and most straightforward) answer is "Because there was no one to make a call."

- [ ] Choice B: We're at the zoo. Perhaps aliens have visited our solar system and Earth but came only to observe. Tech-savvy extraterrestrials probably don't need much from Earth or Earthlings. They don't require our resources—again, space is vast, and they could mine uninhabited planets. Plus, it's unlikely their flying saucers run on fossil fuels. They also don't want our inferior science and tech. They probably developed their own version of the iPhone millions of years ago. They just want to observe us in our natural habitat and don't plan to interfere.

☐ Choice C: Bad timing. Perhaps extraterrestrial beings like our imagined Luigians did visit Earth 80 million years ago and filled up their hard drives with pictures of velociraptors and tyrannosauruses. They might have said to themselves, "Cool planet with awesome beasts, but no one here we can talk to." Then they zoomed off to another part of the galaxy and put Earth on their list of inhabited worlds *without* intelligent, communicating creatures. If aliens were here millions of years ago, it would have been nice if they'd left something, like a time capsule or LONG LIVE LUIGIANS! spray-painted on a mountain.

☐ Choice D: Shhhhh! Aliens might think it's best not to draw attention to themselves. (This follows the logic of choice B.) An intelligent and advanced civilization might not want to make its presence known. In our own short history, we have numerous examples of cultures meeting and clashing, and that's putting it nicely. Aliens keeping quiet could be about self-preservation and avoiding total annihilation.

☐ Choice E: Not worth it. Suppose the Luigians have the scientific knowledge to travel the Milky Way. But someone in accounting put the numbers in a spreadsheet and realized it would cost 90 gabillion schmoopies (that's Luigian currency, obviously), or nearly half the planet's money. The noble citizens voted and decided not to spend the schmoopies. It's not worth it when they could use the funds to end hunger or cure their worst disease. Or maybe the accountant measured the cost in terms of needed energy, and the numbers again didn't look good. Perhaps Luigians believe in preserving their resources.

☐ Choice F: Other: _____. (Fill in the blank.) We can come up with all sorts of ideas for the great silence. Aliens are invisible! They communicate using wawa rays, which humans haven't discovered yet! Aliens are already here, but we just call them armadillos! Or it could be a combination of factors. We just don't know. *Yet.*

While Only Earth–ers are stuck with choice A, Life Beyond Earth–ers can select any other answer. Why didn't the phone ring? The line was cut. The volume was turned off. We left the phone on the bus and missed the call. The caller had the wrong number. Spam blockers silenced the call. Other: _____. (Fill in the blank.)

WHERE ARE YOU?

YOU ARE HERE

(A HANDY GUIDE TO YOUR PLACE IN SPACE.)

You live on Earth and share the planet with
approximately 8 billion other people.

Earth has one natural satellite (meaning: a body orbiting
a planet), and it's called the Moon. It orbits approximately
239,000 miles (384,400 kilometers) from Earth.

Earth is part of a planetary system called the solar system.
There are eight planets and one star (which is called the
Sun) in this system. Earth is third from the Sun.

Your solar system resides in the Milky Way galaxy.
Lots of planetary systems live in the Milky Way,
maybe as many as 400 billion.

The star system closest to you is Alpha Centauri/Proxima
Centauri. You are approximately 4.2 light-years from there.

Andromeda is the nearest large spiral galaxy.
It's about 2.5 million light-years from the Milky Way.

In addition to the Milky Way and Andromeda,
the universe may have as many as 200 billion galaxies.

The universe is expanding.

There is only one known universe.

CHAPTER 2

WHERE DID IT ALL COME FROM?

A HISTORY OF (KNOWN) LIFE IN OUR UNIVERSE

Sadly, all known life in the universe is contained on a single planet that revolves around an ordinary star in the Milky Way galaxy. Not so sadly, life on this rock has resulted in an advanced civilization that can gaze into (not just at!) space, communicate through spoken and written words, and heat a frozen pizza in mere minutes.

Before we continue our journey looking for out-of-this-world life, it would be helpful to know how life started here on Earth. The physics, chemistry, and biology that made you and me possible might also play a role in creating extraterrestrial beings. Or so the theory goes....

SPACE AND TIME

When did it all begin? That's a question scientists and philosophers have been tackling for ages. According to cosmologists, everything (yes, *everything*) kicked off about 13.8 billion years ago with the big bang. From a single infinitely dense and infinitely hot point, the universe emerged and rapidly expanded. It doubled in size ninety times in a fraction of a trillionth of a second. (Or in decimal form, we're talking .0000000000000000000000000001 seconds.) About a literal second later, the universe was home to electrons, neutrons, and protons, but it was dark and would remain that way for hundreds of thousands of years. About 13.6 billion years ago, stars and galaxies began to form during the cosmic dawn, including our Milky Way galaxy, which is a senior citizen in galactic terms. Our solar system is a youngster, just 4.6 billion years old.

These numbers and their impressive collection of zeros can be hard to comprehend. So let's relate time in a more manageable way and scale it down to numbers we can appreciate and wrap our heads around. Imagine each year is only one second long.

Scale: 1 second = 1 year

Event	Real Age in Years	Reimagined in Seconds	That Equals...
Big Bang	13.8 billion	13,800,000,000	437.6 Years
Milky Way Formed	13.6 billion	13,600,000,000	431.3 Years
Our Solar System and Earth Born	4.6 billion	4,600,000,000	145.9 Years
Humans (Homo sapiens) Appeared	300,000	300,000	3.5 Days
You Arrived	Your Age in Years Ex: 13	Your Age in Seconds Ex: 13	Your Age in Seconds Ex: 13 Seconds (You're not even a minute old!)

Curious minds might wonder what was happening 13.81 billion years ago. They might also question where that ultra-dense, ultrahot point came from. At this time, there are scientific theories but no answers. You may also wonder if our universe is the only universe. According to current data, that seems to be the case. Everything we know began with the big bang and exists only in our universe.

Still, we have much to explore! Our universe is expanding and has been since the beginning. Its shape is unknown, and there's no center. The expansion of the universe is often compared to raisin-bread dough. As it bakes, the loaf grows and the raisins spread out. Similarly, the universe grows and the galaxies spread out. But new research shows that this expansion is not the same in all directions. The reason is unknown, but one theory is dark energy (meaning: a theoretical force that opposes gravity—it may or may not exist). Now there are *billions* of galaxies, *billions* of stars, and *trillions* of planets. Astronomers don't know the actual size of the universe, though some estimates put its diameter at 90 billion–ish light-years. From our vantage point on Earth, we can observe only 13.8 billion light-years in any direction. We are limited by the speed of light and the age of the universe.

EARTH: OUR ONE-OF-A-KIND HOME (AS FAR AS WE KNOW)

Life began on Earth within the planet's first billion years of existence. We're not talking about plants or animals but microbes (meaning: microscopic organisms). Unfortunately, fossil evidence from these early years is sparse and doesn't answer the question of how life got started. Therefore, scientists must learn about initial life-forms by experimenting in labs.

You've probably heard the question "Which came first, the chicken or the egg?" If you answered egg, the questioner would ask, "But where did the egg come from?" You'd reply, "From a chicken." The questioner would give an evil smile and say, "But where did the chicken come from?" Around and around you'd go until someone got a stomachache. (Obviously, if you said "chicken" first, you'd still end up in this maddening loop.)

Scientists have the same problem. Life is created from life. But where did the first itty-bitty life come from? In the 1950s, scientists Stanley Miller and Harold Urey developed an experiment to help answer this question. In their lab, they set up equipment to simulate the environment of early Earth. Their glass beakers had only ingredients found on the planet: water, methane, ammonia, and hydrogen. Primordial soup! Then, because storms are part of Earth's early history, the scientists simulated lightning and zapped their ingredients. Miller and Urey waited to see what would happen. Eventually, they had brown sludge in their previously clean environment! This sludge contained amino acids, which are some of the building blocks of life.

Over the years, this experiment has been criticized because a perfect model of early Earth cannot be duplicated in a lab. For example, Miller and Urey used borosilicate glass flasks, which accidentally introduced trace amounts of silica into the experiment. This may have boosted favorable amino acid results. There's also debate about what ingredients were on early Earth and how much of each. However, other scientists have done their own versions of this experiment, and the overall theory holds. Take simple elements, add energy, and get organic, life-building molecules.

LIFE ON EARTH: THE WHAT, WHEN, WHERE, AND HOW

What is life? Biologists (meaning: scientists who study life-forms) can't even agree on a single, perfect definition of life. The best answers are also the longest, and we'd need a few physics and chemistry classes to grasp the concepts. So we'll stick with a basic, oversimplified definition that breaks life down into a list of activities.

Living things do the following:

- Metabolize—the waffles you ate for breakfast are turned into energy and new tissue.
- Grow—you started small and continue to change size and shape.
- Respond—you react to a cold classroom by shivering and complaining.
- Reproduce—biological parents made you, each donating DNA.
- Evolve—your million-years-ago extended family looked a little different because species change through natural selection.

When did life begin? Probably between 3.7 billion and 3.5 billion years ago.

Where did life begin? Somewhere on Earth! (Assuming panspermia isn't the cause—more on this coming up.) Beyond that, the location is up for debate, except it likely occurred underwater. One popular theory has life on Earth beginning deep in the ocean near hydrothermal vents. These chimney-looking structures form as heat and gases escape from Earth's interior (similar to a volcanic eruption), and the temperature surrounding hydrothermal vents can be over 700°F (370°C). Heat is a form of energy. In the Miller-Urey experiment, the scientists simulated lightning to introduce energy into their hypothetical world. But perhaps early Earth life munched on the heat and chemicals from these hydrothermal vents, like tube worms do today.

A second theory doesn't go quite as deep, literally. It suggests that life sprang forth from "warm little ponds," a phrase Charles Darwin (the scientist known for evolution and natural selection) used in a letter to a friend. While there was hardly any dry land 3.5 billion years ago, there were likely areas of shallower water. These pockets allowed molecules to hang out and mingle. A form of energy was introduced (perhaps just sunlight or a zap of lightning), creating more complicated compounds and, eventually, simple life.

How did life begin? Like our title question, possible answers to this question could fill an entire book. It is up for debate, and the truth may forever be unknown. A current accepted theory is that Earth started as an "RNA world." RNA is a chain of chemicals that's able to replicate and carry out functions. Every cell in your body contains RNA and its more complicated cousin, DNA, which provides the directions for that cell to grow, function, and reproduce.

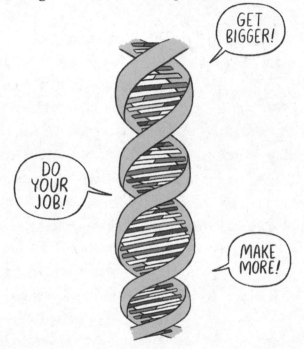

Scientists believe that it took many steps for the world to go from chemicals to cells. Other building blocks of life would be required first. But the rise of RNA—perhaps in warm little ponds or deep in the ocean—looks to have played a significant role.

Or maybe life began through panspermia. This wild theory suggests that life was brought to Earth by space rocks.

Perhaps early comets or asteroids delivered RNA or other genetic material from another world! Evidence of some of life's building blocks has been discovered on asteroids. And microscopic organisms like tardigrades (also known as water bears) can survive in outer space without space suits. Could an early "alien invasion" be why we have plants, animals, and bacteria? Probably not. And if panspermia is behind life on Earth, it still doesn't answer our question of how life began. It just moves the location off our planet.

ALL OUR KNOWLEDGE

Everything we know about life-forms comes from a single sample environment: Earth. Scientists would prefer to study multiple life-hosting planets, but they haven't had that chance yet. This limits some of our thinking and analysis. Imagine it this way: What if everything we know about teams comes from observing the Green Bay Packers (*go, Pack, go!*)? We learn their roster, their plays, their strategies, their strengths, and their weaknesses. We become experts on the Packers—and, seemingly, everything about how a team works. Then, one day, we discover a new team. The Mighty Dragons! They are a small-town kiddie kicker soccer team made up of five-year-olds. The Dragons have some things in common with the Packers. They both have coaches and players (living organisms) and fields of play (environments), but they also have many differences. Like the scoring, the rules, the time of play, the number of participants, the necessary equipment, and the fact that they play *totally* different sports! Studying and observing the Mighty Dragons would change the way we define a team.

Are scientists close to discovering a new "team"? If you are a Life Beyond Earth–er, you probably hope so. In the next chapters, we will check on science's progress.

CHAPTER 3

WHAT'S UP THERE?

THIS CAN'T BE A NEW QUESTION

Things we know to be true and that seem obvious today were mysteries to our ancient ancestors. We now know that Earth is round and revolves around the Sun. We know that the Moon circles Earth and that our solar system has seven other planets. We know that planets even exist outside our solar system. Modern humans are brilliant...especially when we can google things!

At one time in history, humans may have looked up and assumed the stars were distant campfires. The night sky was a mystery, and the theories created to explain the universe do not always fit with our modern scientific models. In fact, the word "planet" is derived from a Greek word that means wanderer, and the ancient Greeks used the term to refer to *all* heavenly bodies: the Moon, the Sun, the stars, comets, and so on. They thought Earth was the center of the universe and that the rest *wandered* across the sky.

Yet, long ago, in a time before telescopes, people pondered whether other worlds might exist. We know that ancient

Greeks, for example, considered this possibility because we have written evidence. It's likely that other groups of people looked at the night sky and also wondered, but their thoughts were not documented in books or TikToks. The oldest ideas on this subject are lost to time.

BELIEVERS VS. NONBELIEVERS

We can lump ancient philosophers and scientists into two camps: those who believed in cosmic pluralism (meaning: that there are worlds beyond Earth that have life) and those who said nope, no way. Basically, the old versions of Life Beyond Earth–ers and Only Earth–ers. The believers included Epicurus, Lucretius, and Metrodorus. Not the most popular Greeks, if you ask me. They're B-level famous at best, but their ideas weren't half bad. Epicurus wrote in a letter to Herodotus:

> There is an unlimited number of cosmoi [worlds], and some are similar to this one and some are dissimilar.

Metrodorus of Chios put it this way:

> It seems absurd, that in a large field only one stalk should grow, and that in an infinite space only one world exist.

Remember, this was when our world was considered the center of everything, with the Sun, the Moon, and the other planets circling our home. These philosophers thought that Earth was the center of the universe. For other habitable worlds to exist, they would need their own universes. *That's a bit mind-blowing and Marvel-movie-like, right? A multiverse!*

The more famous philosophers were Only Earth–ers to their core. Plato and Aristotle thought Earth and Earth alone capable of growing stuff—be it plant, animal, or human. Part of their argument was philosophical, but Aristotle also considered science, which was understood differently at the time. Aristotelian physics had four elements: water, air, earth, and fire. Each element had its place. Water and earth fell to the ground, and fire and air rose up. It went against nature to think that earth and water could be in the sky.

HELIOCENTRIC—NEW AND EXCITING

Before the sixteenth century, the geocentric (meaning: Earth-centered) model of the universe was trendy. The stars, the planets, the Sun, and the Moon circled our beautiful, life-supporting world. But there were some problems with this model. Occasionally, the planets would go the wrong way across the night sky, moving "in retrograde." For example, Mars would sail east to west instead of west to east. Astronomers tried to account for this erratic movement with some pretty complicated models, which all kept Earth at the center of things. The Catholic Church was also a big fan of an Earth-centered universe. It lined up with their views.

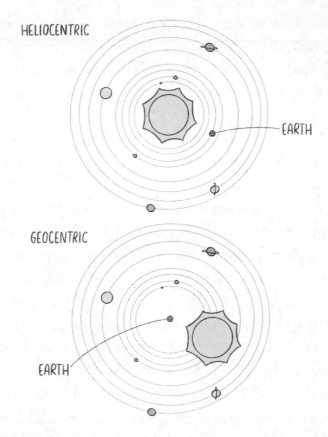

HELIOCENTRIC

EARTH

GEOCENTRIC

EARTH

Then along came a Polish astronomer and mathematician named Nicolaus Copernicus. He put the Sun at the center and suggested that the planets revolved around it. He wrote about this heliocentric model in a small book he initially shared only with friends. It wasn't until he was on his deathbed that the idea was published for wider reading. (The legend goes that he was dying and unconscious but woke when the book was placed in his hands.) Copernicus, who was partly raised by his bishop uncle, dedicated his book to the pope. Maybe Copernicus thought religious leaders wouldn't be upset that he contradicted the Bible if he gave them a shout-out in the beginning. *Clever, right?* And it kinda worked. The Catholic Church did not appear to have strong feelings about the book when it was published in 1543, but it would eventually be banned, in 1616, after the heliocentric model became the *hottest* craze.

Copernicus never had to defend his theory to the church, but years later, Galileo Galilei had to. Galileo took Copernicus's work—which was mostly mathematic and theoretical—to the next level. He created a telescope that magnified the night sky by twenty. He discovered moons around Jupiter, and he was convinced that Aristotle—*Mr. Geocentric*—was wrong. Galileo figured out that the planets revolved in oval paths around the Sun, proving Copernicus right. The Roman Catholic Church didn't like this new science that conflicted with its view of the universe. The church warned Galileo, *Dude, don't go around talking about this.* He obeyed for a while, but then he wrote a book that had info about a Sun-centered universe. He submitted his manuscript to the church censors and got the official A-OK to publish it by putting a note in the front that basically said, "This is all hypothetical, people." But still, others in the church weren't happy. And so Galileo was forced to face the Inquisition (meaning: the church-run court).

Guilty! That was the verdict on whether Galileo had committed heresy (meaning: going against religious opinion), and he was sentenced to prison time. But Galileo was a gentleman and a scholar, which meant he didn't go to a dungeon and wasn't tortured. He "suffered" the rest of his days under house arrest at various villas and apartments in Italy (like when you're sent to your room...but you have a computer there). He continued to study mathematics and science but could not preach his Copernican ways.

The Catholic Church would not accept the heliocentric model of our solar system until 1822. But plenty of people believed it before the church officials gave a thumbs-up to the science. Changing the focus of thinking from Earth-centered to Sun-centered opened minds to new possibilities.

LIFE! IT'S EVERYWHERE!

The eighteenth and nineteenth centuries were good times to be on team Life Beyond Earth. Cosmic pluralism was all the rage. Many scientists, philosophers, writers, and ordinary folk believed that the planets and the Moon were inhabited. There was even a debate about life on the Sun. Thanks to new telescopes, scientists were able to observe sunspots. We now know that sunspots are cooler areas of the star caused by magnetism changes. But back then, William Herschel, the astronomer who discovered Uranus in 1781, thought that these anomalies in the surface were a combination of clouds, oceans, and volcanoes. Even in the 1700s, most scientists disagreed with him. The Sun was too hot and the gravity too strong for any kind of life.

While William Herschel was a self-taught astronomer, his son John benefited from a world-class education, studying mathematics at Cambridge. John would follow in his father's footsteps, becoming an astronomer, and he had access to William's powerful telescopes. *Lucky kid!* In 1834, the younger Herschel went to Cape Town, South Africa, to study the skies from a different hemisphere. Though it was never his intention, his "research" would create a frenzy of excitement.

THE GREAT MOON HOAX

By August 1835, John Herschel had been busy studying the skies from his new location in South Africa for a year. He set up the first telescope observatory south of the equator, and he was there when Halley's Comet passed by Earth, which happens only about every seventy-five years. (Mark your calendar: You can see Halley in 2061!) He'd go on to catalog nearly 70,000 stars and study nebulae and double star systems. What he *didn't* do was observe life on the Moon. But somehow...

Across the Atlantic in New York City, a newspaper called *The Sun* (*ironic, don't ya think?*) was hurting for business—until its new British editor wrote a story about Herschel's recent discoveries. According to the article, Herschel had built the largest telescope ever (it wasn't) and used this new technology to see life on the Moon (he didn't). This wasn't just one fantastical report but a six-day story that grew and caught the world's attention. *The Sun* was no longer a last-place newspaper.

The articles said that the moonscape contained sandy beaches, plenty of vegetation, and pyramids. The Moon was home to exotic creatures, including miniature bison, playful single-horned goats, little zebras, and "Vespertilio-homo" (or man bats)—basically, humans that could fly or glide. *So cool! And so fake!* The editor would later claim that this series about life on the Moon was meant as satire (*calm down, people; it's just a joke*), but not before other newspapers reported on the incredible scientific achievements. The *New York Times* called the discoveries "probable and possible." An Italian newspaper ran impressive lithographs with the story. Not many people were *in* on the joke, though, including John Herschel. *The Sun*'s editor probably selected him as an unwilling participant because John had a famous dad, and John was far away in South Africa.

THE INFAMOUS AND FAKE VESPERTILIO-HOMO

In the end, the story was too good to be true...because it *wasn't* true. But whether it was a stunt to sell papers or a satirical look at the 1800s science community, it did excite readers. Many people were ready to accept the possibility of life beyond Earth. And they wanted proof, just like we still want today.

CHAPTER 4

WHAT HAVE HUMANS ACCOMPLISHED SO FAR?

HISTORY OF THE SPACE RACE

It may seem laughable that people were once convinced man bats lived on the Moon, but that story was well before the space age. Much was unknown. Since then, humans have visited the Moon, remotely flown helicopters on Mars, and sent spacecraft beyond our solar system. Our technological achievements are quite impressive—if we do say so ourselves. Let's take a moment to admire what *Homo sapiens* have accomplished so far. Our past failures and successes might teach us something about future possibilities.

FIRST IN FLIGHT

That's the tagline (or brag-line) on North Carolina license plates. On December 14, 1903, Wilbur and Orville Wright attempted to make history with the first powered airplane flight—but the vehicle stalled on takeoff, and part of it was damaged. *Try and try again!* The brothers fixed the plane and then had to wait for good weather. On December 17, 1903, they accomplished their mission. Orville went first and flew for twelve seconds and went 120 feet (37 meters). (Impressive for sure. But for some perspective, the Boeing 787 Dreamliner, a modern airplane, is 186 feet [57 meters] in length, which is longer than the Wrights' first successful flight.) Then it was Wilbur's turn. He also flew for twelve seconds but covered 175 feet (53 meters). Orville took another turn; this time, he soared for fifteen seconds, traveling 200 feet (61 meters). Not to be outdone, on Wilbur's last attempt of the day, he flew for nearly a minute and covered 852 feet (260 meters). With those four flights, the era of aviation began.

THE MOON GETS A FRIEND

On October 4, 1957, the Moon, Earth's only natural satellite, got some company when the Soviet Union launched Sputnik 1 into orbit. Sputnik weighed about 184 pounds (83 kilograms) and circled Earth once every ninety-six minutes. It stayed in space for three months before plummeting back to Earth. And while in late 1957 our planet had two satellites—the Moon and Sputnik—they were very far apart. The farthest Sputnik traveled from Earth was 584 miles (940 kilometers), while the Moon is over 230,000 miles (370,150 kilometers) away.

SPUTNIK 2: A SAD DOG STORY

Warning: If it's hard for you to read sad dog stories, skip to the next section, "American Pride."

Sputnik 2 launched on November 3, 1957, just a month after Sputnik 1. But Sputnik 2 was special because it carried a dog. Sputnik 1 demonstrated the Soviets' technological superiority over the United States and the rest of the world, and they wanted to keep that reputation intact. The launch of Sputnik 2 was hasty with the goal of putting an animal in space for the anniversary of the Russian Bolshevik Revolution. The Soviet team found a 13-pound (6-kilogram) mutt living on the streets of Moscow. At first, they called her Kudryavka, which means Little Curly, but later her name was changed to Laika, which means Barker.

Sputnik 2 weighed about six times more than Sputnik 1. It had a small cab for Laika with enough room for her to sit or lie down. Laika's compartment also contained a video camera, a water and food dispenser (her meals were served in gelatinized form), an oxygen system, a harness restraint, and devices for monitoring the dog. Officially, Laika's voyage was an experiment to see what would happen to creatures in space.

The Soviet scientists never intended to bring Laika back to Earth. The technology for that wasn't yet available. The Sputnik 2 cabin had enough oxygen, food, and water for a ten-day mission. Laika did not live that long. The mutt survived the launch, and initial Soviet reports said she died painlessly a week later. This was propaganda. Laika may have lived a few days (which is the current Russian stance on the subject) or only five or six hours. Severe panic and overheating likely killed her because the thermal systems failed, and portions of Sputnik 2's insulation were destroyed during launch.

Side note: The United States did not use dogs as stand-in astronauts, but it did use primates such as rhesus monkeys and chimpanzees. In June 1948, a rhesus monkey named Albert died of suffocation on board a US V2 rocket. Officially, Albert did not enter space; he reached only 39 miles (63 kilometers) of altitude. (The space line is arbitrary but often considered to be 100 kilometers.) Many other monkeys—named Albert II, Albert III, and so on—were also sacrificed for space science.

AMERICAN PRIDE

The success of Sputnik 1 and the audacity of Sputnik 2 surprised many Americans. The United States had grown accustomed to being a leader in technology and innovation: first in flight, the Manhattan Project (which created nuclear bombs), air-conditioning, the microwave oven, and the flyswatter. But when it came to space exploration, the USA was falling behind—and falling behind to an old ally and new enemy, the USSR. On December 6, 1957, the US attempted to play catch-up by launching an uncrewed (no dogs, no apes, no people) satellite, but the Vanguard rocket exploded immediately after takeoff, and the failure earned the nickname Kaputnik. Luckily, the United States had other rocket programs in the works. They'd get another chance soon.

On January 31, 1958, the US successfully sent up its first satellite, Explorer 1. The teams that designed and built the satellite and modified the Jupiter-C rocket (which was originally intended for nuclear missiles) completed their tasks in a mere eighty-four days. Explorer 1 orbited Earth about 12.5 times per day and remained functional for 112 days, collecting data about cosmic rays. It was the first satellite to make a scientific discovery!

Other Explorer missions that year would find success *and* failure.

- Explorer 2—March 5, 1958—Failure: Jupiter-C rocket did not ignite properly
- Explorer 3—March 26, 1958—Success
- Explorer 4—July 26, 1958—Success
- Explorer 5—August 24, 1958—Failure: Rocket boosters collided

SPACE IS FOR THE DOGS (NOT A SAD STORY)

The Soviets were moving closer and closer to sending a person into space. To test the feasibility, they again used dogs—and some other animals. The Sputnik 5 capsule carried two dogs (Belka and Strelka), forty mice, two rats, and a rabbit. Their adventure launched on August 19, 1960. Like the cabin in Sputnik 2, this capsule contained a camera. Scientists watched Belka and Strelka carefully, and during the first three laps around Earth—each of which took ninety minutes—neither dog moved. But then, on the fourth lap, Belka vomited, and both dogs seemed to wake up. The animal crew completed seventeen orbits total and then successfully returned to Earth. When their cabin was opened, the dogs seemed happy and healthy. They became celebrities, appearing in magazines and newspapers and on TV. Strelka would also become a mom, and one of her pups, Pushinka, would be a gift from the USSR to President Kennedy and his family. (The FBI made sure to check the puppy for tiny microphones and other spy gear. No joke.)

FIRST MEN AND ONE WOMAN

The Soviets had sent dogs to space, and the Americans had launched primates. It was time for humans to experience the thrill and danger of a launch.

- Yuri Gagarin (Soviet)—April 12, 1961—First man in space and first to orbit Earth
- Alan Shepard—May 5, 1961—First American in space but did not orbit
- John Glenn—February 20, 1962—First American to orbit Earth
- Valentina Tereshkova (Soviet)—June 16, 1963—First woman in space and first woman to orbit Earth

AMERICAN PRIDE, PART II

If anyone was keeping score—and they were totally keeping score—the Soviets were winning. For many Americans, this hurt their red-white-and-blue pride but also scared them. The space race was happening during the Cold War, when countries were developing bigger, nastier nuclear weapons capable of killing millions with the press of a button. (It's slightly more complicated than a button, but not by much!) If the Soviets had better space equipment—namely rockets—they probably had better weapons too. Americans needed to get super serious about space to disprove any inferiority.

In May 1961, US president John F. Kennedy made a now famous speech, challenging America to put a man on the Moon by the end of the decade. (Man on the Moon seemed to be the arbitrary finish line.) He said:

> We choose to go to the Moon. We choose to go to the Moon in this decade and do the other things, not because they are easy, but because they are hard, because that goal will serve to organize and measure the best of our energies and skills, because that challenge is one that we are willing to accept, one we are unwilling to postpone, and one which we intend to win, and the others, too.

Kennedy's speech is great and inspiring; you can watch it online. Not only did he speak with conviction, but he also backed NASA and the mission with funding. The race was *really* on now!

SOVIETS (SPACE)WALKING INTO THE LEAD

Soviet Alexei Leonov took the first spacewalk on March 18, 1965. And by spacewalk we mean he went outside his capsule. Leonov floated in space for twelve minutes. Things didn't go smoothly. His space suit ballooned because of the effects of space's vacuum, and he had to deflate it manually, which resulted in decompression sickness. Eleven weeks later, American astronaut Ed White took his own spacewalk. On June 3, 1965, White floated outside the Gemini IV spacecraft.

The first spacecraft to land (not crash) on the Moon was also Soviet. Luna 9 touched down on February 3, 1966. Its success proved that the Moon had a solid surface and that vehicles would not get swallowed up in layers of dust. The United States' first lunar landing was on June 2, 1966, and Surveyor 1 sent back more than 11,000 pictures over the next month.

SPACE EFFECT

As we've seen, early spacecraft were not crewed by *Homo sapiens*. Scientists did not know what would happen to the human body (or animal body) when it experienced weightlessness. Without the gravity we are accustomed to, would our eyeballs pop out of their sockets? Would we be able to digest food, or would astronaut ice cream sit in our esophagi? How would blood circulate through arteries and veins? Of course, we had to wonder how we'd excrete poop and pee.

NASA now has a department called the Human Research Program (HRP). It's responsible for the research and technology used to keep astronauts safe. In March 2015, the agency had a unique opportunity to study a set of identical twins—one twin stayed on Earth while the other spent 340 days on the ISS. Over the course of the mission, scientists noted some differences between Scott Kelly (the brother in space) and Mark Kelly (the Earth-bound brother). Scott's body mass decreased, and fluids shifted from his legs to his upper body. The shape of Scott's eyeballs also changed (though they did not fall out), and his carotid artery wall became thicker. Other irregularities were noted in Scott, but his body mostly went back to normal when he returned to Earth. If *Homo sapiens* are going to settle on the Moon or voyage to Mars, these types of experiments will be crucial for the safety of astronauts. It would not be wise to establish homes in far-off places without understanding how the human body reacts.

SPOILER: THE US WON THE SPACE RACE

If we consider sending a man to the Moon to be the finish line, the USA won on July 20, 1969. Neil Armstrong, followed twenty minutes later by Buzz Aldrin, was the first person to land on the Moon and walk on the surface. (Michael Collins was also on this mission but was essentially forced to wait in the car. He did not leave the command module.) As Armstrong stepped onto the lunar dust, he said, "That's one small step for man, one giant leap for mankind."

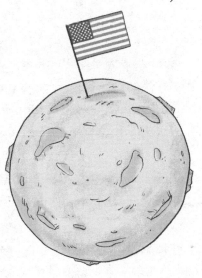

The Soviet Union never sent a human to the Moon. Actually, as of this book's publication date, no other country can claim this honor.

OTHER WORLDS

Sure, the Moon is awesome, but it's relatively close, and NASA and its Soviet counterpart also sought to explore farther reaches of our solar system. Through the end of the century, these two countries (and others) would shoot for the stars, and onetime enemies would even collaborate and live together on space stations.

Mariner 4 (USA): Launched November 28, 1964. After an eight-month-long journey, Mariner 4 completed the first successful flyby of Mars. *(Yes! You read that correctly. NASA sent a spacecraft to Mars before an astronaut walked on the Moon.)* Mariner 4 captured twenty-one images of the red planet during a twenty-five-minute window. It took about ten hours to transmit each picture back to Earth. No aliens were spotted. (Much more on Mars missions in Chapter 6.)

Salyut 1 (USSR): Launched April 19, 1971. Meet the world's first space station. It was designed to house three cosmonauts (meaning: Soviet or Russian astronauts) for two months at a time. The first attempt to populate the vessel failed when a hatch wouldn't open. On the second attempt, the crew stayed for twenty-three days, but tragically they died on their return to Earth.

Mars 3 (USSR): Launched May 28, 1971. Good news! The Soviets successfully set down the first lander on Mars. Bad news! Contact was lost with the lander after twenty seconds.

Pioneer 10 (USA): Launched March 2, 1972. For this mission, NASA looked to visit the giants of our solar system. Pioneer 10 was the first spacecraft to go past the asteroid belt (that space-rock-filled lane beyond Mars), and it successfully flew by Jupiter (its objective), collecting pictures and data. No aliens were spotted.

Skylab (USA): Launched May 14, 1973. NASA's first space station also housed three people and required repairs immediately. One of the main goals of Skylab was to study how the human body handled space, specifically low gravity and perceived weightlessness. The final crew stayed aboard for a record-setting eighty-four days.

Venera 9 (USSR): Launched June 8, 1975. This successful journey to Venus took over four months. The Venera 9 lander operated for only fifty-three minutes, but it captured a 180-degree picture from the Venusian surface—the first picture ever taken *on* a non-Earth planet! (The image was supposed to be a 360-degree range—a full circle—but one of the camera covers didn't come off like it was supposed to.) No aliens photobombed the pics.

Viking 1 and Viking 2 (USA): Launched August 20, 1975, and September 9, 1975. The Viking landers were the first American spacecraft on Mars, and their little life-hunting experiments caused excitement—and controversy—back on Earth. (We'll see the results in Chapter 6.) While the goal was for the landers to operate for ninety days, Viking 1 sent transmissions for more than six years. Viking 2 lasted over three and a half years.

Voyager 2 and Voyager 1 (USA): Launched August 20, 1977, and September 5, 1977 (yep, they were launched "out of order"). These spacecraft are like the Energizer Bunny: They keep going and going and going....On August 25, 2012, Voyager 1 became the first human-made object to reach interstellar space. It left our solar system! Voyager 2 took its time and achieved the same feat on November 5, 2018. On their way out of the neighborhood, these twins explored Jupiter,

Saturn, Uranus, Neptune, and forty-eight of their moons. Voyagers 1 and 2 also carry the Golden Record (more on this in Chapter 9).

Columbia (USA): Launched April 12, 1981. Columbia was NASA's first space shuttle, which is a partially reusable vehicle that can carry people, equipment, and cargo. The 1981 Columbia launch blasted off without major issues. But, decades later, on February 1, 2003, Columbia was returning to Kennedy Space Center after its twenty-eighth mission when it exploded. The seven astronauts on board were instantly killed.

Hubble Space Telescope (USA and ESA, European Space Agency): Launched April 24, 1990. All photographs taken by Earth-based optical telescopes have some level of distortion because of the atmosphere. Hubble was the first optical telescope set into orbit around Earth, giving humans new and spectacular images of space. It has not captured pictures of aliens. (More on Hubble in Chapter 12.)

International Space Station, or ISS (Collaboration): The first piece of the ISS, the Zarya Control Module, took off for space on a Russian Proton rocket on November 20, 1998. The United States would send its first piece, Unity (AKA: Node 1), on December 4, 1998. The inaugural crew consisted of one American and two Russians and arrived in November 2000. Initially—way back in the '80s—the ISS was a US-only project named Freedom. In the '90s, it turned into a group project, with Russia becoming a major team player and other countries joining in (Canada, Japan, Brazil, and eleven countries in the European Space Agency). Teamwork makes the dream work! The ISS is still operating, though political conflicts are changing the landscape—or space-scape.

Disappointingly, none of these space expeditions have led to discoveries of alien life. In nearly all cases, that was not the aim anyway. But these scientific accomplishments (and the many, many not listed here) are moving us closer to answers about life beyond Earth. In the next chapter, we'll take a close look—like, a needing-a-microscope look—at the small stuff that might be lurking in our own solar system.

CHAPTER 5

WHAT WILL WE FIND?

LIFE IS ABOUT THE SMALL STUFF

Imagine this headline: "Alien Life Found!" (and assume it's not satire from *The Sun*). Such news would be trending everywhere: on TV, on social media, and on your bus ride. This would be a big moment for science and for Life Beyond Earth–ers. Maybe the biggest in our lifetime! But chances are this tantalizing headline will not be referring to intelligent, technology-loving, bigheaded green aliens. Small stuff is probably more common in outer space. It certainly is on Earth.

HUMANS ARE OUTNUMBERED

The *Homo sapiens* population is over 8 billion, up from around one billion just 200 years ago. So our species seems healthy and prosperous. Other large animals aren't doing as well.

African Elephants = 415,000-ish

Chimpanzees (our closest relatives) = fewer than 250,000

Polar Bears = nearly 26,000

Black Rhinos = around 5,500

Tigers = about 4,500

Giant Pandas = under 2,000

If we focused on just these numbers, it would seem like we are the most populous of critters. But chickens outnumber humans. (There are about 33 billion of them, mostly raised for food.) And though no one goes around counting rats or mice, they're easily in the billions and likely exceed the human population. But these figures don't even begin to tell the whole story of life on Earth. One teaspoon of productive soil will contain hundreds of millions of bacteria—maybe even a billion. In my gut alone (just me, the author), there are 100 trillion bacteria that come in hundreds of species.

The small stuff rules planet Earth, but we sometimes forget because we can't see it without a good microscope. This might be true for other places in our galaxy and even in our local solar system. Astrobiologists think several spots in our galactic neighborhood might be potentially hospitable to teeny-tiny life-forms.

While alien life could be very different from what we know, chemistry principles can still lead us in our search. Earthly life-forms need water, are carbon-based, and consume stuff. In general, astrobiologists are on the hunt for these three things.

- Water
- Chemical elements
- Energy

But where shall we look?

PLANETS AND DWARF PLANETS

In general, scientists have ruled out the giants of our solar system—Jupiter, Saturn, Uranus, and Neptune. They're just not hospitable to life as we know it. The temperatures, atmospheric pressures, and ingredients are all wrong. Of the four rocky planets, we know that Mercury is too close to the Sun. It's hot and flooded with solar radiation. That leaves only a few places to investigate.

Venus: This planet is known as Earth's twin because they're similar in size. However, they have very different environments. Venus is hot enough to melt lead and is under high pressure. The thick cloud-like atmosphere lets little sunlight through to the surface. And while there may have been an ocean billions of years ago, out-of-control greenhouse gases have heated the environment, and all the water has evaporated. Basically, the planet's surface is horrible for life. Yet some scientists would like to take a closer look at Venus's yellowy cloud of atmosphere. High up, the environment has less pressure and a more hospitable temperature and contains life-forming ingredients. Looks like Venus's atmosphere meets two of our three potential-life requirements (chemical elements and energy from the Sun), but what about H_2O? *Nope.* According to new research, there's just not enough water vapor to support even the most drought-tolerant microbes.

Mars: *Hold that thought!* Mars will be discussed at length in the next chapter.

Pluto: This dwarf planet—please don't come at me about its official title—is frozen and ridiculously far from the Sun, but still, it could have a liquid water ocean beneath its frozen exterior. And, as we've learned, life on Earth began in the sea. Pluto also has a thin atmosphere of mostly nitrogen. (Earth's atmosphere isn't thin, but it is mostly nitrogen.) The odds are slim that life exists here, but wouldn't that be sweet revenge on Pluto's part if this former planet was home to microorganisms?

Ceres: This dwarf planet is located in the asteroid belt. It was considered the largest asteroid until it got promoted to dwarf planet status. Though it's small—about a quarter of the size of our Moon in volume—scientists get excited over

Ceres because it has water. Well, ice. Under its rocky surface is a thick layer of frozen H_2O, and there's proof of water vapor in its atmosphere. Ceres may actually have more water than Earth! And in 2017, the NASA spacecraft Dawn discovered signs of organic compounds. It's all so exciting. Unfortunately, Ceres doesn't have a great energy source for supporting life. It's too far from the Sun, and there doesn't seem to be geothermal activity (meaning: heat and energy coming from within the planet/dwarf planet/moon).

MAYBE A JOVIAN MOON

According to NASA, Jupiter has a swarm of eighty moons. The four biggest—Europa, Io, Ganymede, and Callisto—each have a different environment, and some may have the potential for primitive life.

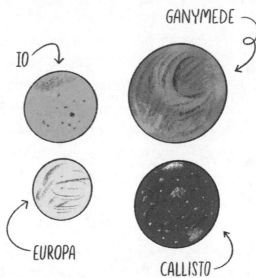

Europa: Smaller than our Moon, Europa is covered in miles and miles of ice. But beneath its frozen outside, there's likely a salty ocean. Europa has water. *Check!* Assuming it has a rocky core, Europa could have the necessary chemical elements. But what about energy? The Sun's light is not going to penetrate all that ice. But Europa may have volcanic vents that spew hot gases—similar to the hydrothermal vents in our oceans. Organisms may be able to feast on this energy. According to NASA, Europa might be our best bet for finding life-forms in our solar system.

Io: This moon is a happening place, at least for geological activity. For starters, there are over 400 active volcanoes. The moon's surface also rises and falls like our oceans' tides. In some spots, the low-to-high change is 330 feet (100 meters). Io certainly has energy. *Check!* But it seems to lack water; it's just too hot! We're unlikely to find organisms here.

Ganymede: This giant moon is the largest in the solar system. It's bigger than Pluto and even Mercury. Like Europa, Ganymede is cold and covered in an icy shell. Beneath the ice, there's likely a salty ocean and a rocky core. It's also the only moon with a magnetic field, which is vital for diverting harmful solar radiation. Ganymede gets to check all three boxes for organism potential. *Go, Ganymede!*

Callisto: Jupiter's second-largest moon (and our solar system's third-largest) has a rocky, icy surface marked by impact craters. For decades, Callisto was considered the boring

CRUNCHY OUTSIDE WITH LIQUID CENTER

Several moons have liquid oceans beneath their icy or rocky surfaces. These oceans remain in liquid form not because of the Sun and not because of a hot, fiery core. It's because of tidal heating (also called tidal flexing). On Earth, ocean tides are affected by the gravity of a close object (the Moon) and a big object (the Sun). Similarly, the subterranean ocean on the Jovian moon Europa, for example, is pushed and pulled on by Jupiter—and Jupiter is both large and close. This movement creates heat through friction and keeps the subterranean ocean from freezing.

moon because it has no volcanic activity or erosion (meaning: the wearing away of surface material). Basically, the exterior of this moon hasn't changed much and looks the same as it did when our solar system formed 4.6 billion years ago. (The impact craters are new additions, of course. Asteroid collisions can happen at any time.) But after a NASA mission in the 1990s, scientists now wonder if this moon has an ocean underground. If it does, it's really, really deep—155 miles (250 kilometers) deep. An ocean—whether subterranean or exposed to the surface like on Earth—is exciting because of its potential for life.

MAYBE A NON-JOVIAN MOON

Jupiter isn't the only planet with interesting, consideration-worthy moons.

Titan: Saturn's largest moon and, in our solar system, second only to Ganymede, Titan has liquid on its surface. We're talking rivers and lakes. Titan also has an atmosphere made mostly of nitrogen, which Earth can also claim. But before we point all our telescopes in this direction in search of plants and animals, we should understand that Titan is still quite different from our planet. Those rivers and lakes are not made of H_2O. On Titan, it rains methane and ethane (which are types of natural gases that humans use for fuel). The moon's surface pressure is also 50 percent greater than on Earth. But beneath the surface might be a water ocean. We know that spells potential. Titan could have Earth-like life in its underground ocean and some very un-Earth-like life on the surface—not the carbon-based life-forms we're used to.

Enceladus: Another of Saturn's moons and another bitter-cold spot in our solar system, this ice-covered moon has a watery ocean beneath its surface. But Enceladus is different because the water continuously shoots through the ice and into the atmosphere like a geyser. NASA spacecraft have witnessed this awesome phenomenon. Some of these icy particles rise high enough to become part of Saturn's rings! Most float back down like snow onto Enceladus's surface. Astrobiologists believe this moon has all the ingredients for potential life, including energy from hydrothermal activity. And thanks to these sprays into the atmosphere, spacecraft can collect and analyze samples of the subsurface ocean.

ENCELADUS GEYSER

Triton: This frozen moon of Neptune is not on the top of the list for potential life, but it should still be considered because of its geological activity. It may have that all-important under-surface ocean, and it does have geysers that spit out liquid nitrogen, methane, and other particles—all of which instantly freeze. It's unlikely there's life on Triton, but it's an active place worthy of a closer look.

Finding teeny-tiny life-forms in our solar system would be incredible and headline-worthy no matter where they're located. In the next chapter, we'll explore Mars—perhaps the place we're most likely to find organisms—and we'll also dive into the human obsession with Martians.

CHAPTER 6

MAYBE MARS?

SPOILER: NO MARTIANS BUT
STILL MUCH TO PONDER

Mars can be seen with the naked eye, and thus a telescope was not required for its discovery. That's how the ancients knew of the red planet, and the Romans named it after their god of war because of its bloody coloring. For centuries, this small, cold planet has held a special place in the human imagination. Many have looked into the night sky and wondered what the inhabitants of our neighboring world might be like.

Martian enthusiasm got a boost in 1877 when Italian astronomer Giovanni Virginio Schiaparelli, using a telescope, observed straightish lines on the planet's surface. Schiaparelli also noted dark spots, which he labeled Martian seas, and light spots, which he assumed were continents. But it was the lines he called *canali* that drew excitement. English speakers mistakenly translated that Italian word into "canals" (meaning: artificial waterways) and assumed the *canali* were constructed by Martians, just like the Erie Canal and the Suez Canal were made by Earthlings. *Canali* actually translates to "channels," which are natural structures, and Schiaparelli never meant to imply that they were created by anything but nature. But plenty of people preferred the Martian-made idea.

It turns out that the 100-plus straight lines Schiaparelli and other astronomers observed in the nineteenth century were illusions. The limited viewing power of the telescope and natural elements on Mars's surface—like craters and canyons—caused the appearance of the *canali*. Also, a trick of the human brain is that it seeks out patterns and will create them even when there are none. But one American man embraced the canal theory with gusto and devoted much of his time and wealth to proving the existence of life on Mars.

MEET PERCIVAL LOWELL

Percival Lowell was born to a wealthy family in Boston, Massachusetts, in 1855. In his early adult years, he traveled and studied literature, but when he learned about Schiaparelli's *canali*, he became a man on a mission. In 1894, Lowell built his own private state-of-the-art telescope in Flagstaff, Arizona, and began his observations of the red planet, complete with piles of drawings. Lowell believed that the canals carried water from Mars's polar ice caps to the planet's equator. The dark markings around the canals, he thought, were vegetation—maybe signs of farming. These canals were more impressive than any found on Earth: According to Lowell's measurements, they ran for thousands of miles, or as Lowell put it, "as far actually as from Boston to San Francisco."

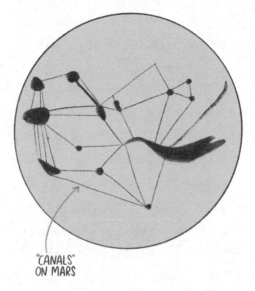

"CANALS"
ON MARS

Lowell wrote several books about Mars, including *Mars and Its Canals* (published in 1906). Other astronomers immediately began debating Lowell's claims. They simply did not observe these canals. But Lowell never backed off, and his ideas caught on with the general public. His "findings" were published in newspapers around the world.

Also around the turn of the twentieth century, Mars stories flourished in fiction. In 1897, H. G. Wells published the science-fiction story *The War of the Worlds* about a Martian attack, which kicked off the alien invasion genre. And the classic green-skinned Martian image came from a book, *A Princess of Mars* by Edgar Rice Burroughs (first serialized in 1912). People were enthusiastic and open-minded about green life on the red planet, in both fiction and nonfiction books.

One of the most infamous Mars stories occurred in 1938.

(Lowell missed this event. He died in 1916, still convinced about canals and intelligent life on Mars. The man would not be dissuaded.) The 1930s were a time before YouTube and even before television. Radio shows dominated home entertainment. Families could gather around the radio for news, fictional stories, or music. One regular program was *Mercury Theatre on the Air* (no association with the planet). On this show, actors performed popular books like *Treasure Island* and the Sherlock Holmes series. For the broadcast on October 30, 1938, Orson Welles and the rest of the cast would act out *The War of the Worlds*. But Welles and the writers worried that the story was dry and dull, so they decided to up the drama. They'd make the first act sound like a breaking-news bulletin. (You've probably seen those on television, when a newscaster interrupts your regularly scheduled programming with a report about something awful.) At the beginning of the radio show, it was announced that the following story was fictional, that Martians were not currently invading New Jersey. But families who tuned in a few minutes late would have missed that important announcement. The next forty minutes were filled with eyewitness accounts of citizens being terrorized by Martians. The space invaders used a mysterious weapon that the reporters called a heat ray, and poisonous black smoke overtook Newark.

During the description of the invasion, there were no commercial breaks or other interruptions to the story. So people believed that Martians had really destroyed New

Jersey. Some called the police. Some hid. Later, there would be reports of listeners even dying by suicide, but that was not true. The next day, Orson Welles found himself in the middle of a controversy. Reporters—real reporters—wanted to know if Welles had meant to terrify listeners. Had he intended for them to think the broadcast was real news? At the time, he claimed he'd never meant to cause panic.

The story of this infamous broadcast has ballooned over the years. Some estimates say that 12 million Americans listened in, but other reports say that less than 2 percent of those with radios heard Welles's broadcast because another, more popular show was on a different channel at the same time. It was the newspaper reports in the following days that made the story—and alien invasions—infamous.

The canal debate (and the resulting intelligent-life-on-Mars debate) would not be put to rest until the 1960s, when NASA's Mariner missions captured better images of the planet. As you probably know, Mars lacks canals, pyramids, roads, skyscrapers, malls—or anything a Martian engineer might design. It also did not appear to have forests or oceans, which was somewhat expected but still disappointing. The *New York Times* ran an editorial titled "Dead Planet." Yet, regardless of the *Times* piece, scientists couldn't say for sure whether the planet was utterly lifeless.

VIKINGS GO LOOKING FOR LIFE

By the 1970s, the world knew that Mars lacked plants and animals. But what about microorganisms? To find out, NASA included three experiments aboard Viking 1 and Viking 2 to determine if the Martian soil contained teeny-tiny life. One of these was the labeled release (LR) experiment, which essentially involved taking a dirt sample and adding water and organic material. If the sample contained microbes, they'd devour the organic material and create some kind of waste product that could be measured—like carbon dioxide or methane gas. The experiment ran as intended, and the apparatus sent the data back to labs in the United States. The results were positive for life. *Wahoo!* This was it! This was the moment Life Beyond Earth–ers dreamed of.

Unfortunately, the two other experiments on those same Viking missions did not find evidence of life. That made many scientists take a closer look at the LR experiment, beginning a debate that still exists today. Some astrobiologists believe that a chemical reaction—not tiny living critters!—could have caused the positive results. (Like when you make a volcano in your kitchen using baking soda and vinegar. That's a chemical reaction, not waste from a living organism.) The official NASA stance is nope, the LR results aren't confirmation of life on Mars. Or, in NASA's own words in 2016:

> The science team believed the LR data had been skewed by a non-biological property of Martian soil, resulting in a false positive.

Still, some of the scientists who designed the equipment think differently. They'll have to agree to disagree until we have more data.

JUMPING TO CONCLUSIONS

Lowell and friends thought they had evidence of Martian life at the end of the 1800s. *Strike one for life on Mars.* Some astrobiologists thought they had evidence in the 1970s. *Strike two!* Surely the world wouldn't make hasty judgments a third time. *Right?* Well, it seems it's just too easy to get our hopes up. (If I may speak on behalf of the Life Beyond Earth–ers, "We want to find aliens!") So we shouldn't be surprised that in August 1996, when *USA Today* boldly declared, "The headline man has been waiting for since the first human eyes looked into the heavens," it was another jump-to-conclusions moment.

The story begins on Antarctica in 1984. Scientists routinely travel the icy landscape looking for meteorites (meaning: rocks from space). This environment is a great place to search because anything not white will stick out in the snow and ice. (Looking for space rocks in a forest, field, or body of water is much more difficult, if not impossible.) In December, researchers discovered meteorite ALH84001, a rock that wouldn't get much attention for another decade. In 1993, scientists determined that ALH84001 was from Mars and was over 4 billion years old. Turns out that a crash on the red planet about 16 million years ago sent debris into the solar system, and this meteorite sailed through space before landing in Antarctica. *So cool!*

Then NASA geochemists analyzed ALH84001 and found a few exciting things. First, they saw orange specks made of carbonite. On Earth, carbonite forms in water from the fossilized shells and skeletons of critters. Did this mean Mars had liquid water? Did this mean decaying Martian species caused the carbonite? Second, scientists found strange, tiny, wormlike shapes that resembled bacteria but smaller. Following these discoveries, a team of scientists closely examined the rock for over three years and concluded that the microscopic evidence showed potential for early Mars life. (Not exactly concrete proof. Just potential.) They published a paper about their findings to much excitement. It even got the attention of the White House. On August 7, 1996, President Bill Clinton addressed the world.

> Today, rock 84001 speaks to us across all those billions of years and millions of miles. It speaks of the possibility of life.

Other scientists almost immediately began to counter these ideas. *Hold on! Not so fast! This rock doesn't tell us much about possible Martian life!* All the elements and signatures in ALH84001 could be attributed to non-biological formation. And research published in 2022 confirms that the interesting elements in ALH84001 are not a product of ancient Martian life. So once again, eager humans had their hopes dashed.

THOSE CUTE LITTLE ROVERS

NASA continues to feverishly study Mars by sending spacecraft, rovers, and even drones to the red planet. It's a top destination for uncrewed missions. *(No humans yet!)* Scientists are learning more about our neighboring planet, including about its potential for life—past or present.

Mars Pathfinder: Landed July 4, 1997. The lander and the rover (named Sojourner) were sent to Mars to collect soil, rocks, samples of the atmosphere, and climate info. This mission found pebbles near the landing site, which scientists believe were formed by running water. It's possible Mars was warm and wet in its ancient past. Much different from the frozen sphere it is today.

Mars Polar Lander: Dead on arrival December 3, 1999. This mission was supposed to drill into the polar region of

Mars to search for water ice. NASA lost contact with the lander on its entry into Mars and never heard from it again. A report years later determined that the lander crashed due to a problem with its sensors. *Oopsie!*

Mars Exploration Rovers: Spirit landed on January 4, 2004, and Opportunity on January 25, 2004. These roving geologists checked out two different sites on the planet. Both locations were chosen because they potentially had watery pasts. Spirit found evidence of long-dormant volcanic activity, impacts from space, and subsurface water, as well as patches of salty soil that point to possible ancient H_2O. Opportunity discovered signs of long-ago lakes. Both adorable rovers were meant for ninety-day missions, but they outdid themselves. Spirit worked for over six years, and Opportunity sent its last transmission on June 10, 2018, nearly fifteen years after launch.

Mars Phoenix: Arrived May 25, 2008. This lander set down in a region of the planet farther north than any other mission had explored. Phoenix used a probe to collect soil from a two-inch-deep (five-centimeter-deep) trench in Mars's arctic. The lead scientist summed up the result: "We have water. We've seen evidence for this water ice before... but this is the first time Martian water has been touched and tasted." *Who's thirsty for more?* (For the record, the probe did the tasting, not the scientists. We've yet to return specimens from the red planet.)

Curiosity: Landed August 6, 2012. This still-in-use rover was tasked with finding evidence that Mars once had the potential to foster life. And according to NASA, this *curious* mobile science lab "found chemical and mineral evidence of past habitable environments on Mars." Basically, Curiosity's data collection says, *Yeah, it's possible, but we still don't know for sure.*

Perseverance: Touched down on February 18, 2021, along with the first Mars helicopter, Ingenuity. Percy's official jobs are to look for signs of ancient microbe life and to collect rock and soil samples for future missions to bring back to Earth. Percy is quite a photographer (pictures can be found on the NASA website) and is also conducting experiments that may someday help prepare astronauts for living on the red planet.

SPEAKING OF MARS EXPLORATION

These NASA robots are amazing and gather vital information, but perhaps the best discoveries will come when we send humans to Mars. Which begs the question, when will that be?

NASA's current plan starts with Artemis. Here's how the Artemis website describes the program:

> With Artemis missions, NASA will land the first woman and first person of color on the Moon, using innovative technologies to explore more of the lunar surface than ever before. We will collaborate with commercial and international partners and establish the first long-term presence on the Moon. Then, we will use what we learn on and around the Moon to take the next giant leap: sending the first astronauts to Mars.

The exciting program is underway. Artemis I successfully launched an uncrewed mission to test new rocket technology in November 2022. Artemis II will take astronauts on a journey around the Moon, farther from Earth than humans have ever gone before. Artemis III will involve a Moon landing and the US's first return to our natural satellite in over fifty years. This historic event is planned for sometime in 2025. From there, the hope is to build an Artemis base on the Moon's south pole. This establishment will be a publicly and privately funded multinational operation. The Moon base will be a testing ground for the technology we will need to walk on Mars one day. And when will that be again? NASA aims to send astronauts to Mars in the late 2030s or early 2040s, but the Artemis program is already running behind schedule. And funding might be more of an issue than technology.

NASA is not the only space agency that's gung ho about planetary exploration. China also recently announced its intentions to send a crew to Mars in 2033 (and again in 2035, 2037, and 2041). In 2021, China sent its first rover to the planet.

Our fascination with Mars is alive and well—though it's no longer driven by the search for canals or big-eyed, green-skinned creatures. One day, Mars may be an astronaut destination, and one day, it may reveal its secrets about microorganisms (past or current).

CHAPTER 7

WHAT ABOUT NOT~ FROM~THESE~ PARTS PLANETS?

EXOPLANET DISCOVERIES

In case you haven't created a diorama of our solar system recently, let's review the major players. A 4.6-billion-year-old G-type yellow dwarf star, which we affectionately call the Sun, resides at the center. Orbiting this star are eight planets. Most of these planets have moons. (Mercury and Venus don't have any, and Earth has just one.) There are also five dwarf planets, an asteroid belt filled with over a million space rocks, and, at the far reaches of the system, the Kuiper belt, which is loaded with icy rocks and maybe more dwarf planets.

Even with all these exciting locations across the solar system, life has been found only on Earth. Maybe scientists will someday discover microscopic life beyond our planet, but if we want to rub elbows with *intelligent* life (would they have elbows?), we'll certainly need to leave our galactic neighborhood.

So, let's go.

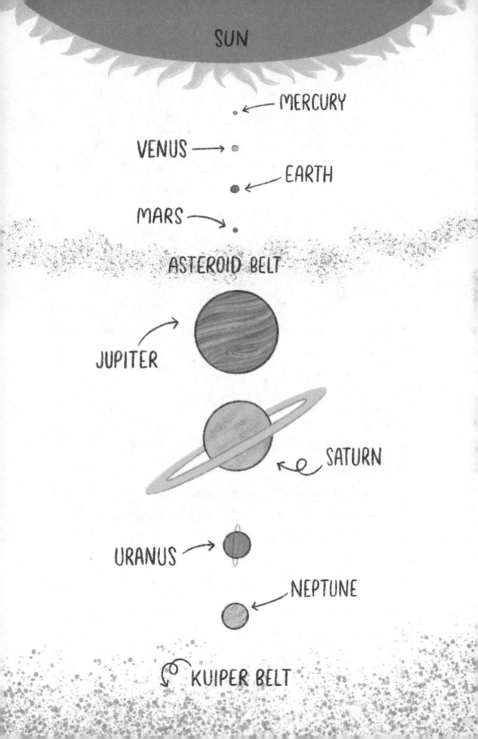

EXOPLANETS

To put it simply, exoplanets are planets outside our solar system. Astronomers have speculated about their existence for decades, even centuries. Think of it this way: Humans have known for thousands of years that those twinkling lights in our night sky are stars. And since our favorite star (the Sun!) is orbited by planets, why wouldn't at least some of those billions of stars have the same setup we've got here? But it wasn't until 1992 that astronomers proved that exoplanets are a thing.

Since that first discovery, over 5,000 exoplanets have been confirmed, and more than 9,000 are waiting to join the club. (Scientists like to prove and double-check information, but that takes time and leads to a long exoplanet confirmation wait list.) Finding exoplanets isn't easy—or astronomers would have done it long ago. The telescopes that can see Jupiter, Neptune, and other objects in our solar system cannot zoom in on exoplanets. They're just too far away. Luckily, astronomers have different tools for exoplanet hunting.

Transit Method: A telescope measuring the light of a distant star will notice a dimming when an orbiting exoplanet passes by. *Bingo! Exoplanet discovered!* With this method, alignment is crucial between the telescope, star, and exoplanet. Imagine a bug flying in front of a streetlight. We'd need to be standing in the right place (and have very sensitive equipment) to notice it. This method is responsible for approximately 75 percent of confirmed exoplanet discoveries (as of 2022).

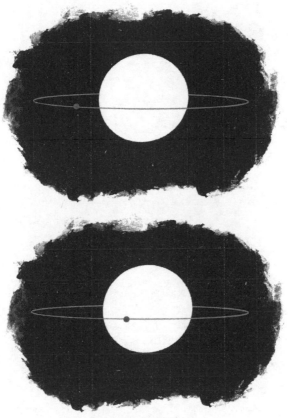

TRANSIT METHOD

Radial Velocity Method (or Wobble Method): Stars have gravity. Planets also have gravity—this is what keeps you from flying off Earth's surface. The bigger an object, the more gravitational force it exerts. That's why planets orbit stars and not vice versa. But planets, especially big planets, can still affect their stars, pulling on them and causing a wobble. Telescopes can observe this wobble. The radial velocity method is responsible for about 20 percent of confirmed exoplanet discoveries.

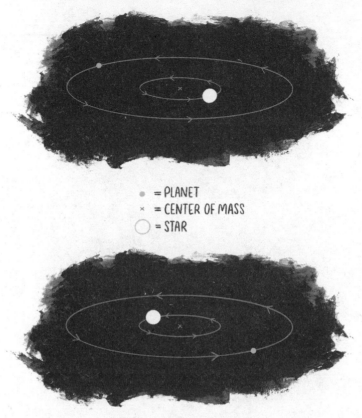

= PLANET
× = CENTER OF MASS
◯ = STAR

RADIAL VELOCITY METHOD

Gravitational Microlensing: When an exoplanet passes between a distant star (not the star it's orbiting) and an observer with a telescope, the light from the distant star bends—just like light bends in the lenses of a pair of glasses. But this warping of light is caused by gravity, not glass. Gravitational microlensing is best for discovering the farthest exoplanets and is responsible for less than 3 percent of confirmed exoplanet discoveries.

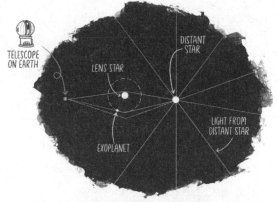

GRAVITATIONAL MICROLENSING

Direct Imaging: Stars are bright. Planets are not. For a high-powered telescope to take a picture (capture a direct image) of an exoplanet, the star's light must be blocked. This method is best for exoplanets that have large orbits and that are closer to our solar system. New technology is being developed for this type of search (see starshades in Chapter 12). So far, few exoplanets have been discovered using direct imaging. This method is responsible for approximately 1 percent of confirmed exoplanet discoveries.

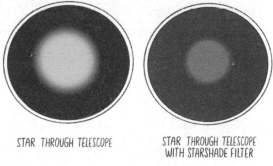

STAR THROUGH TELESCOPE   STAR THROUGH TELESCOPE
                          WITH STARSHADE FILTER

DIRECT IMAGING

FLAVORS OF EXOPLANETS

Using current techniques, astronomers can determine an exoplanet's distance from Earth, orbital time (meaning: the exoplanet's year length), and size. With further study, scientists might learn about the planet's temperature, density, and atmosphere—which are important for hypothesizing about life potential. NASA has established categories to help sort through these far-off planets.

Terrestrial: These are the smallest exoplanets but can still be up to two times Earth's size. (Mercury, Venus, Mars, and Earth are terrestrial planets in our solar system.) Terrestrials are rocky and likely have an iron core. Their surface can be solid or liquid, and some may have a gassy atmosphere.

Super-Earth: These exoplanets are two to ten times bigger than our home planet and could be rocky, icy, or both. Our solar system does not have any super-Earths. Sometimes, the exoplanets on the big side of this range are called mini-Neptunes.

Neptunian (or Neptune-Like): Exoplanets in this category are like Neptune or Uranus in size. (It would be more fun if NASA called these Uranusian or Uranus-like, *don't ya think?*) In our solar system, we often refer to Neptune and Uranus as ice giants. However, Neptunian exoplanets can be cold or hot. They can be covered in a cloudy atmosphere or have clear skies. Neptune-like exoplanets are the most common exoplanets past a star's snowline (meaning: in the zone where water remains permanently frozen).

Gas Giant: The last category is for the big guys. In our neck of the woods, these would be Jupiter and Saturn. However, much larger exoplanets have been discovered. Gas giants typically have a solid core surrounded by dense gases—hence the name. Since Jupiter is five times farther from the Sun than Earth, and Saturn is about nine and a half times farther, it was thought that gas giants didn't like to hang out too close to their stars. But discoveries over the past decades—often using the wobble method of detection— show that this is not true. Gas giants can orbit in a range of distances around their stars.

STRANGE NAMES

How do exoplanets get their names? With over 5,000 confirmed and so many more waiting to be discovered, we can't use only characters from Greek mythology. Naming planets usually begins with naming the star they revolve around. (Except for rogue planets, which are planets without a star to orbit.) A star can be named after its location, the telescope or program that made the discovery, or the person behind the find. Being the biggest and brightest object in the system, the star is discovered first and gets the letter A attached to the name. If it's a multi-star system, letters B, C, and so on can be used. Once exoplanets are found and confirmed, they get the star's root name and the next letter alphabetically. Because the letters are assigned in order of discovery date, technically, a D planet could be closer to its sun than a B planet. The letter does not tell us the planet's distance from the star. A list of exoplanets can be found at https://exoplanets.nasa.gov/discovery/exoplanet-catalog.

THIS PLACE SEEMS NICE: WHAT ARE WE LOOKING FOR IN A DREAM EXOPLANET?

Imagine you live in this strange town where the only fruit available is oranges. Everyone eats oranges. You have oranges at meals and for snacks. Your favorite recipes call for freshly squeezed oranges. It's all you know. Then you travel to another town and stop at a store, where I give you a few bucks and say, "Do me a favor. Go inside and buy me some fruit." You'll probably walk up and down the aisles looking for oranges because that's what is familiar to you. You might wander right past lemons, strawberries, and bananas (they're not even close to the right shape!). It's all you've ever known, so it's what you seek out.

When scientists analyze an exoplanet and try to determine if it's ideal for life, they often look for the factors that have made Earth awesomely livable. Life could thrive in other conditions too, but we know what works at home. The following is a wish list for an ideal exoplanet.

(Some of this data can be determined with our current technology. A lot of it cannot.)

- **Habitable Zone:** This is the region around a star where liquid water can exist on the surface of an orbiting planet.

(Obvs, Earth hangs in the habitable zone of the Sun.) It's also called the Goldilocks zone because it's not too hot (so that all water would evaporate) and not too cold (so that all water would freeze). *It's just right.* Finding an exoplanet in the habitable zone seems to be at the top of the must-have list for a life-supporting home. When a Goldilocks exoplanet is located, this detail makes it into headlines: "New Exoplanet Discovered in Habitable Zone." As exciting as it may be to find such a planet, it doesn't mean there will be life or even liquid water. In our solar system, Venus is at the inner ring of the habitable zone, and Mars is on the outer edge; neither has known life. Our Moon is also in the ideal neighborhood, and it's mostly dust and rock.

· **Star Type:** Only the right kind of star will do. Our Sun is a stable G-type yellow dwarf. It's not too hot, not too cool, and not too violent. Astronomers are looking for G-type yellow dwarfs, but there might be other stars that are even better suited for hosting habitable planets. The life span of G stars is on the shorter side, cosmically speaking—about 10 billion years. K-type orange dwarfs are cooler but might be better hosts because they can shine on for tens of billions of years and don't emit high levels of ultraviolet radiation. A long-living star might mean a long-living extraterrestrial species.

· **H-2-YO!** Perhaps it's possible to have life without water, but that is not the case on our home planet, which is 71 percent water. We know that life on Earth likely began in H_2O and that cells need water, but also, our gigantic ocean is vital for Earthling existence: It helps maintain global temperatures, makes oxygen, and provides a home to 15 percent of all Earthly life. Currently, scientists aren't able to determine whether an exoplanet has an ocean, but water vapor has been detected in some instances, and one study that used mathematical modeling suggested that more than 25 percent of exoplanets could have oceans (either on the surface or beneath ice or rock).

- **Atmosphere:** Earth is wrapped in a sweet blanket of gases (AKA: an atmosphere), which is mostly made up of nitrogen (78 percent) and oxygen (21 percent). Nitrogen is an unreactive gas—it minds its own business and doesn't get involved with other gases. Not only would an exoplanet with plenty of O_2 (AKA: oxygen) have life-making potential, but it would also be a safe-ish place for us to visit. (However, a lack of oxygen does not necessarily mean a lack of life.) Earth's atmosphere provides insulation, helping maintain the planet's temperature and protecting us from solar radiation and smaller asteroids (which burn up in the mesosphere, though occasionally pieces do land on our planet's surface; those are called meteorites). The composition of an exoplanet's atmosphere can sometimes be determined with the transit method, but not all exoplanets are found with this technique, and it can be time-consuming.

- **Tectonic Plates:** Crust is good on pizza and on planets. Earth's outer surface is made of constantly moving tectonic plates. (Imagine a cracked shell on a hard-boiled egg.)

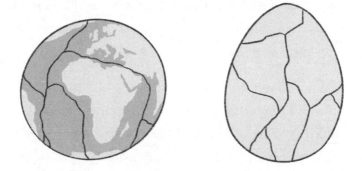

Plate tectonics are vital for maintaining temperature over millennia, controlling carbon dioxide in the atmosphere, creating diverse landscapes, and triggering volcanic activity, without which a planet would probably be too cold for organisms. Earth is the only planet in our solar system—currently—with tectonic plates and the only planet with life. *Coincidence?* (That said, there may be other ways for an exoplanet to maintain temperature and control gases in the atmosphere.) Plate tectonics are nearly impossible to determine on far-off planets, though a team of scientists used computer modeling to find strong evidence of plate tectonics on LHS 3844 b. Unfortunately, this exoplanet is not in the habitable zone and doesn't have an atmosphere.

- **Size:** Not too big and not too small. Massive exoplanets have a mighty gravitational pull and can hold on to lots of gases in their atmosphere. Too many, really. It becomes a thick, gassy soup. However, a very small exoplanet would not have the gravitational pull to keep its atmosphere—the solar winds would blow the good gases away. It also would be unable to hang on to its water. Terrestrial and smaller super-Earth exoplanets are in the ideal size range.

- **A Natural Satellite:** Our Moon is not just important for werewolf legend. It prevents Earth from wobbling on its axis, which keeps our climate stable. Without our large and close satellite, Earth would tilt, and instead of the Sun being *above* the equator, it could slowly move over millions of years to be in line with the poles. *Talk about climate change!* Now, if a supervillain like Gru and his Minions were ever successful in stealing the Moon, Earth life would suffer greatly: no high and low tides, which are vital to many ecosystems; a darker night sky that would mess with nocturnal animals' rhythms; and goodbye twenty-four-hour days—Earth's rotation would speed up. In addition to our Moon, there are over 200 other moons in our solar system. (Even dwarf planet Pluto has five.) So it's likely many exoplanets have moons as well. Our current technology cannot easily detect them, though there are a few possible exomoons being investigated.

- **Core:** It's what's inside that counts. And we're not talking about an exoplanet's heart. Scientists would like to find an exoplanet with a spinning iron core (like Earth has), which is important for creating a protective magnetosphere (meaning: an area around a planet where magnetic fields dominate). It acts like a defense system, helping shield a planet from radiation from the local star and cosmic rays from deep space. This is important for keeping a water-rich atmosphere. Scientists sometimes can predict whether an exoplanet has a solid core if its precise radius and mass are known.

- **A Pleasant, Stable Temperature**: A lot of this comes down to habitable zone, star type, atmosphere, and geology (ocean, plate tectonics, core). But temperature is still worth mentioning on its own. Think about Earth. Plant and animal life is more diverse and plentiful in warm, wet spots than in cold, dry locations. And climate stability gives lifeforms time to mature and prosper. Again, thinking about Earth, we know that animals can go extinct when their natural habitat experiences climate change. Exoplanet temperatures cannot be directly measured, though some researchers have made estimates.

It's worth repeating: Our exoplanet wish list is based on what we know works in our solar system. *(It's like we're looking for oranges, or maybe grapefruit.)* And what works in our solar system is Earth and only Earth. If astrobiologists could find a planet that meets all (or even most) of this list, it certainly would make Life Beyond Earth–ers optimistic.

STAR LIGHT, STAR BRIGHT, STAR TYPE

Categorizing stars is not a simple task. Scientists want to know a star's size (including mass, volume, radius), temperature, luminosity, color, and age, along with other, complicated details. Astronomers have developed various classification systems to sort through the stars. The charts below are simplified but will help us understand terms used in this book.

Temperature and Color

Temperature	Letter	Color
Hottest	O	Blue
	B	Blue-White
	A	White
	F	Yellow-White
	G	Yellow (Our Sun!)
	K	Orange
Coolest	M	Red

Size and Brightness

Classification	Radius	Luminosity
Supergiant	30 to 500 times greater than our Sun	Most Luminous Up to 1,000,000 times greater than our Sun
Giant	10 to 50 times greater than our Sun	
Main Sequence (AKA: Dwarf)	Between one-third the size of our Sun and 10 times greater	
White Dwarf	1% the size of our Sun	Least Luminous

A star spends most of its life cycle as a main sequence star. It's in its prime, fusing hydrogen into helium (AKA: nuclear fusion). Main sequence stars can be smaller or bigger than our Sun, and they also vary in brightness, temperature, age, and color. They're quite diverse! Once a main sequence star runs out of hydrogen, it will transform into a supergiant, giant, or white dwarf (or other subcategory) depending on the star's initial size.

On the flipside, Only Earth–ers can use the exoplanet wish list to highlight our home planet's awesomeness (and uniqueness). Life on Earth seems dependent on these criteria, and astronomers have yet to find another place like it in the universe.

LIKELY CANDIDATES, MAYBE

A safe estimate is that there are billions of exoplanets in our Milky Way galaxy alone. Yet NASA has confirmed only about 5,000 so far. We have a lot of work ahead of us. Still, some of these exoplanets have more life-hosting potential than others—and maybe even have the potential to support the supersmart kind of life (the kind that would play *Roblox*).

(Reminder: One light-year is the distance light travels in a year—about 5.88 trillion miles, or 9.46 trillion kilometers.)

HD 28185 b: In 2001, the first exoplanet in a Goldilocks zone was discovered. This gas giant is nearly six times bigger than Jupiter. *Wowzers!* It orbits a G-type star like our Sun, and it's 128 light-years from Earth. Just because it's in the right place doesn't mean HD 28185 b is the best candidate. It is considered uninhabitable—way too big, lots of gravitational pressure, and a dense, gassy environment.

Teegarden's Star b: This super-Earth exoplanet is speedy. It takes less than five Earth days to revolve around its star. It orbits in the habitable zone of a gentle red dwarf, a good and unusual star type. (Most red dwarves are volatile and hotheaded, spewing powerful solar flares that can damage an atmosphere.) We don't know if Teegarden's Star b has an atmosphere or much else. It's twelve light-years from us. Hopefully, new technology will allow us to find out more about this potential life-hosting planet.

TOI 700 d: This exoplanet is also a super-Earth orbiting in a habitable zone around an M-type red dwarf. It was the first discovery by NASA's Transient Exoplanet Survey Satellite (TESS). This exoplanet is probably tidally locked (meaning: it revolves and rotates at the same speed, so the same side of the planet always faces its star). Imagine if half of Earth always received the Sun's light and the other half never was illuminated. Life might still be possible, but not the life we know. Again, more data is needed to determine if TOI 700 d has an atmosphere.

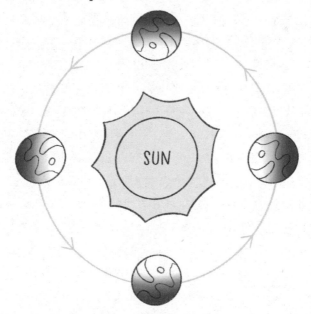

Proxima Centauri b: So close, yet so far. This is our nearest exoplanet, just over four light-years away. While it is in the habitable zone (yay!), its M-type star emits ultraviolet radiation hundreds of times more powerful than our Sun's (boo!). Lots of UV radiation can be atmosphere-destroying because it strips away all the gases. It's unlikely that Proxima Centauri b is habitable.

Kepler-452b: From a NASA press release in 2017: "NASA's Kepler mission has confirmed the first near-Earth-size planet in the 'habitable zone' around a sun-like star." Is this the exoplanet we've been dreaming of? Technically, Kepler-452b is a super-Earth, about 60 percent larger in diameter, and older, about 6 billion years old. (Reminder: Earth is 4.54 billion years old.) A year on Kepler-452b is 385 days, just twenty days longer than an Earthly year. Does this potential life host have an atmosphere, water, a rocky surface? Don't know. And since it's 1,400 light-years away, it'll be a while before we get additional evidence.

TRAPPIST Planets: Also in 2017, astronomers told the world about the magnificent seven of TRAPPIST-1, a planetary system about forty light-years away. Planets TRAPPIST-1b, c, d, e, f, g, and h are all relatively Earth-sized and in our favorite habitable zone. More study is necessary to determine whether these exoplanets have liquid water and a suitable-for-life atmosphere. Still, seven possibilities are better than one.

KOI 5715.01: In 2020, researchers at the University of Washington created a list of criteria for labeling exoplanets as "superhabitable." *The best of the best!* The researchers consider these places even more perfect for sprouting life than Earth. (It's pretty apparent that Earth is perfect enough for sprouting life, though.) Here's what they came up with:

- Orbits a K-type dwarf star
- Approximately 5 billion to 8 billion years old
- Up to 1.5 times more massive than Earth and about 10 percent larger than Earth
- A temperature about 8°F (5°C) warmer than Earth (which is ironic, because if Earth's temperature rose by 8°F, humans would be in trouble, if not extinct)
- An atmosphere with water vapor, 25 to 30 percent oxygen, the rest unreactive gases
- Smaller continents scattered about with lots of shallow water
- A moon that's large (1 to 10 percent of the planet's mass) and not too far away
- Plate tectonics and a geomagnetic field

Of the thousands of known exoplanets, the researchers put twenty-four on their superhabitable list. Unfortunately, all the candidates are at least 100 light-years away. KOI 5715.01 is the top choice because of its age (5.5 billion years old), size (approximately two times Earth's diameter), star (an orange dwarf), and potential greenhouse gases (to lock in needed heat). It's ripe with possibility! *Yay!* But it's 2,965 light-years away. *Bummer!* Still, for Life Beyond Earth–ers, finds like this are cause for excitement and hope.

THE FUTURE IS BRIGHT

Scientists are desperate for additional data about these far-away planets. Thanks to new technology and programs, we'll not only find additional exoplanets, but we'll learn more about them. For example, the James Webb Space Telescope (JWST), launched in December 2021, will use spectroscopic instruments to examine the atmospheres of these distant worlds. (More on the JWST in Chapter 12.) Perhaps one (or 100 or 1,000) exoplanets will be superhabitable in actuality and not just in theory. We could be only a couple of years away from finding an exoplanet with liquid water or an oxygen-rich atmosphere! Each discovery moves us closer to answering our question about life beyond Earth.

CHAPTER 8

DO CALCULATORS HOLD THE ANSWER?

LET'S LOOK AT THE MATH

What do you do when you don't have the answer to a problem? Ask a teacher? Ask a librarian? Ask your adult at home? Ask Google? Sometimes, no one has the definitive answer, so we turn to math to evaluate the probability of solutions. Meteorologists do this every day. Even with the best equipment, they cannot absolutely predict tomorrow's weather. Instead, they give the chance of rain or snow in percentages and the accumulation in ranges. And if you're hoping for school to be canceled, it stinks when they incorrectly forecast a huge snowstorm that ends up being a dusting.

Other scientists do this as well. With so much unknown in our universe, astronomers have turned to math to predict answers to our burning question about aliens. And, it turns out, both Life Beyond Earth–ers and Only Earth–ers can use numbers to prove their assumptions.

DR. DRAKE AND HIS FAMOUS EQUATION

The year was 1961, and the location was Green Bank, West Virginia. For months the previous summer, a young Frank Drake had been listening to two nearby stars, hoping to pick up radio waves from an advanced civilization. He came up empty-handed. (More on this in Chapter 9.) Drake's efforts didn't capture proof of aliens, but they did capture the attention of the National Academy of Sciences. This organization asked Drake to assemble a team to discuss the search for extraterrestrial intelligence (SETI). It was time to take the hunt for aliens seriously.

The world's first SETI meeting took place over three days in Green Bank and began on Halloween. Drake was in charge of the guest list and invited ten men, including a soon-to-be Nobel Prize winner, Melvin Calvin, and a young Carl Sagan, the man who would go on to create the popular show *Cosmos*. (No women or people of color were at the meeting. This stinks but was common at the time because few non-white men were admitted to study in the STEM fields.)

Before the Green Bank conference started, Drake realized he needed some structure for this event. He quickly—so the legend goes—came up with an equation to examine the possibility of alien life. He never meant for this formula to be solvable. It was a conversation starter. A conversation that continues sixty-plus years later.

Meet the Drake Equation:

(Does this look like a fun tattoo? Lots of people have gotten this formula permanently inked on their bodies. You can also just buy it on a T-shirt.)

POSSIBLE SOLUTIONS FOR AN EQUATION WITH NO SOLUTIONS

Drake and his colleagues never thought they'd solve the equation. That wasn't the point. Still, it's a fun exercise to guesstimate numbers. So let's do it.

N—Number of Technology-Loving Civilizations in Our Galaxy. This is the solution to the equation. Basically, how many planets with ETI (extraterrestrial intelligence) are out there?

R_*—Star Formation Rate. As we know, our Milky Way galaxy is about 13.6 billion years old, which is old old old. It's had a lot of time to birth stars, and its most productive years seem to be in the past. But still, new stars are forming in the Milky Way, and the estimated rate varies from one to seven new stars per year. For our mathematical demonstrations, we'll go with three.

$$R_* = 3$$

f_p—**Fraction of Stars with Planets.** The group certainly thought exoplanets were possible, but the proof was still over thirty years in the future. For a time, it was believed that stars with planets might be special. Now astronomers know they're the norm. Like people with cell phones—it seems everyone has got one. Let's be optimistic and say that all stars—100 percent of stars—have planets. (In fraction form, 100 percent is 1/1, or 1.) Though a new study suggests that not every star has an exoplanet, the research still maintains that there are as many planets as stars in the Milky Way.

$$f_p = 1$$

n_e—**Number of Planets in a System Capable of Life.** Let's look local. The number of planets in our solar system with life is one. The number of planets *capable of* supporting life could be argued (as we've seen with Mars and Venus). A 2020 study found that stars could have as many as seven Earth-sized planets in their Goldilocks zone. Let's pick a number between one and seven.

$$n_e = 3$$

f_l—**Fraction of Habitable Planets with Life.** Of all those planets with the right climate, the right atmosphere, plenty of water, and a plethora of organic material, what fraction would sprout life? Many biologists believe that if you have all the ingredients for life, it's inevitable. Life will find a way. It might even be 100 percent guaranteed. Let's be optimistic and go with a value of one.

$$f_l = 1$$

f_i—**Fraction of Planets with Intelligent Life.** The next consideration is *intelligent* life. Of course, we mean smart like us *Homo sapiens*. Plenty of Earthly animals are considered smart, from the elephant to the octopus to the crow to my dog Ray-ka (but not my dog Munchkin). But we want to find the true brainiacs capable of complex language, advanced communication, and abstract thought. Most scientists lean toward a low value for f_i. The thinking is that we humans are pretty unique. Of the millions of species inhabiting our planet, only one has ever *considered* the existence of extraterrestrials. Crocodiles have been roaming for millions of years longer than us, yet they have not evolved into a species that can read, write, or contemplate what exists beyond our planet. Let's say only 10 percent. (Ten percent is 10/100, which is .1.)

$$f_i = .1$$

f_c—**Fraction of Technologically Capable Planets.** We're contemplating intelligent beings who've developed technology that can be transmitted into space, whether on purpose (messages sent into the cosmos) or by accident (radio waves leaked into space as a byproduct). Sure, humans are "f_c compliant" now. But look back at our early ancestors: The only way an alien civilization could have seen them was if the aliens got close enough to spot cooking fires. This is going to be a low number. Let's say 1 percent (which equates to 1/100, or .01).

$$f_c = .01$$

L—Average Lifetime of a Technologically Capable Civilization. For how long would a technology-loving space-broadcasting civilization be able to stick around? There are two extremes to this debate. On one side, it could be argued that such a species will stick around forever because of its awesome ability to solve problems and fix things. (That would be nice.) On the flip side, it could be argued that these beings will eventually create weapons capable of destroying themselves and everything around them. Or that they'll destroy their world through mismanagement of resources. Looking at our planet, a case could be made for both situations. (Read my book *Save the People!* for more about this topic!) If advanced creatures don't stick around long, there's a chance we could miss our sister civilization, like ships (or spaceships) passing in the night.

Homo sapiens have been at this level of technological sophistication for less than 100 years. So let's be reasonably optimistic and say that the average life span of a technologically advanced civilization is 10,000 years.

$$L = 10{,}000$$

Time to start calculating. What do we come up with using our reasonable (but still nonscientific) numbers?

$$N = R_* f_p n_e f_l f_i f_c L$$
$$N = 3 \times 1 \times 3 \times 1 \times .1 \times .01 \times 10{,}000$$
$$N = 90$$

According to our guessing, there are ninety planets in the Milky Way capable of communicating.

We can tweak our thinking and numbers and get very different results. For example, if we say civilizations last, on average, a million years, then...

$$L = 1{,}000{,}000$$
$$N = R_* f_p n_e f_l f_i f_c L$$
$$N = 3 \times 1 \times 3 \times 1 \times .1 \times .01 \times 1{,}000{,}000$$
$$N = 9{,}000$$

While the equation was not meant to be solved, Drake and his associates did plug in some numbers: $R_* = 1$, $f_p = .2$ to $.5$, $n_e = 1$ to 5, $f_l = 1$, $f_i = 1$, $f_c = .1$ to $.2$, $L = 1{,}000$ to $100{,}000{,}000$.

Using the low-range numbers:

$$N = 20$$

Using the upper limits:

$$N = 50,000,000$$

If you grab your own calculator, you can make your best guess, and the answers can vary widely.

As a mathematical certainty, the Drake equation is kinda worthless. Both Only Earth–ers and Life Beyond Earth–ers can use it to argue their side. Too many unknowns! But as a conversation starter—especially if it's tattooed on a forehead—it's brilliant.

A TRILLION IS A LOT

There are hundreds of billions of stars in the Milky Way galaxy. That's a lot! But there might also be billions of *galaxies*, all with as many stars—potentially. That's a lot a lot! Considering there might be a trillion planets out there, it's a little self-centered to imagine that Earth is the only one with awesome beings. (Sorry, Only Earth–ers. I'm not trying to throw

shade.) But one scientist believes that a trillion might not really be a lot if we reframe our thinking.

Astronomer Stephen Webb takes a closer hypothetical look at these trillions of potential habitats in his 2018 TED Talk. He blatantly states, "We're alone." Obviously, there's no absolute proof that we are, but he has his own mathematical way of explaining his Only Earth–er beliefs.

Critters like us—clever and curious about the cosmos—faced many barriers (or hurdles) to come into being. Many things had to go just right for you and me to be here. It would be tedious (and probably impossible) to give scientifically calculated odds to each barrier. So for simplicity, Webb gives each barrier a 1-in-1,000 chance. This is truly a guesstimate. Like asking, "What are the chances someone would make a half-court shot in basketball?" Seems 1 in 1,000 is a fair guess. Sure, give me 1,000 tries to sink the shot, and maybe I'll get lucky once. An NBA player would probably score several times. A toddler wouldn't get any baskets.

Numerical Starting Point:

Chance of jumping each hurdle: 1 in 1,000

Possible number of planets in our galaxy:
1,000,000,000,000 (that's a trillion)

Bring on the barriers! (Some of this will sound familiar. You may experience a little Drake equation or Fermi paradox déjà vu.)

That first hurdle is habitability. A place in the Goldilocks zone with the right mix of water and life-building elements. If each planet has a 1-in-1,000 chance of having these things, we divide 1 trillion by 1,000 and now have a billion contenders left.

1,000,000,000,000 ÷ 1,000 = 1,000,000,000 POSSIBLE PLANETS IN OUR GALAXY

The second hurdle is climate stability. Earth has had approximately 4 billion years of decent weather. We talked about some of the reasons why in Chapter 7: a marvelous Moon, tectonic plates, an iron core, and an electromagnetic sphere. Sticking with our 1-in-1,000 odds, we're now down to a million possible planets.

1,000,000 POSSIBLE PLANETS IN OUR GALAXY

Even in the right conditions, will life actually form? (And we know that scientists aren't in consensus on how it even began on Earth.) Keeping with this simple math, Webb uses the 1-in-1,000 barrier, and we're down to a thousand.[1]

1,000 POSSIBLE PLANETS IN OUR GALAXY

Next, consider the jump to complex life: from single-celled organisms to smart animals like dolphins, crows, and us. We are now down to one planet in our galaxy. (Yay, Earth!)

1 POSSIBLE PLANET IN OUR GALAXY

But there are additional hurdles Webb wants us to consider. Like planets with beings that develop sophisticated tools. If 1 in 1,000 can do this, then we are looking for one planet in a thousand galaxies.

1 PLANET IN 1,000 GALAXIES

These aliens don't just need tools; they need complex math and science. Again, assuming 1 in 1,000 is capable...

---

1   In his talk, Stephen Webb admits that his 1-in-1,000 odds are not proper calculations or based on scientific data. As noted in our discussion of the f_l value in the Drake equation, many biologists believe that life is inevitable given the right ingredients and environment. There may also be dozens of other hurdles or barriers that stand in the way. Like with the Drake equation, it's not the calculations that are most important; it's the conversations that can be spurred by considering the numbers.

1 PLANET IN 1,000,000 GALAXIES

Add in a structured society able to communicate complicated thoughts and work together for common goals; we're looking at one in a billion.

1 PLANET IN 1,000,000,000 GALAXIES

It would also be good if this complex, intelligent, math-loving society avoided catastrophes. They need the environment to be kind (a long-lasting star, no major asteroid collisions, a lack of natural disasters), and they also need to not destroy themselves for a long while. That's one in a trillion.

1 PLANET IN 1,000,000,000,000 GALAXIES

This rough math estimates that one planet in all the galaxies is technologically advanced and able to communicate across space. That one planet would be Earth. A thought that is both miraculous and scary.

A REAL PARADOX

Again, we don't mean a couple of physicians. It doesn't matter what equation we use to consider the probability of alien life. We know the universe is incomprehensibly huge. I could give analogy after analogy to try to help us wrap our heads around this idea.

- If the universe were a herd of elephants, our solar system would be a flea on one elephant's back.
- If the universe were a grassy field the size of Colorado, our solar system would be a blade of grass.
- If the universe were a dictionary, our solar system would be a single letter on a random page.

Regardless of what lousy analogy you'd like to use, we have to agree that the universe is enormous, and we can barely contemplate it. And, since it's so large, it might seem ridiculous to believe we are alone. That's what Life Beyond Earth—ers would likely say: There's no way this is all a lifeless void.

So where does the paradox come in? If we agree that the universe is enormous, do we also agree that finding life in the hugeness is nearly impossible?

- Could you find your pet flea if she jumped onto the back of one of the elephants?
- Could you find a particular blade of grass in Colorado?
- Could you find the *correct* single letter in the dictionary?

The universe is enormous; there's no way we can be alone. But also, the universe is enormous; there's no way we'll bump into anyone else (or hear anyone else or see anyone else).

Or if you prefer the good ole needle-in-the-haystack analogy...

FIND THE NEEDLE!

OR NEEDLES.

OR MAYBE THERE'S NO NEEDLE...

BUT FEEL FREE TO LOOK!

MAKING HEADS OR TAILS OF THIS

When you flip a penny, what do you get? Heads or tails. Right? But is there a third, rare option? Could the penny land on its smooth edge? A penny can certainly be balanced on its edge. (Try it! As a matter of fact, I just did.) So, given enough chances, a penny *might* land in a vertical position. Personally, I've never seen this happen. Maybe that's the situation with Earth. With each planet, the universe flipped a coin, and heads is hot and hostile, and tails is cold and cruel. Then there's the edge. The nearly impossible. We already know that Earth is incredible. We're going to need more data and better tech before we know whether Earth is *uniquely* incredible.

CHAPTER 9

DID YOU HEAR THAT?

SETI TIME

Let's think like Life Beyond Earth–ers and assume extra-terrestrials exist. They're out there—somewhere. And probably far, far away. Given everything we know, our first conversation with these aliens will not likely be face-to-face. *(Should we even assume aliens have faces?)* We are much more likely to spot them from a great distance, at least initially. That's what SETI scientists are working on: looking and listening for signs of intelligent life—but mostly listening.

In 1959, two Cornell scientists wrote a groundbreaking paper titled "Searching for Interstellar Communications." It was the first time that *listening* to specific types of electro-magnetic waves had been suggested. (See page 108 for info about waves.) Their research showed that radio waves travel well in space, passing through gas and dust without inter-ference. The scientists suggested an ideal frequency range, which some have nicknamed the "water hole," for communi-cating across the galaxy. (The thought was that any advanced civilization would know about this ideal range.) The researchers hoped that alien civilizations were purposefully using these wavelengths when communicating with their galactic neighbors. Perhaps they would even be sending messages specifically for us.

DUDE, RIDE THE WAVES!

Quick physics lesson! Light is a wave. Often when we talk about light, we focus on visible light. *ROY G. BIV!* Our eyes can perceive only the waves in a narrow section of the electromagnetic spectrum. But most light waves fall outside this little colorful band. The type of light wave depends on the size, or wavelength, which is measured from crest to crest (or peak to peak).

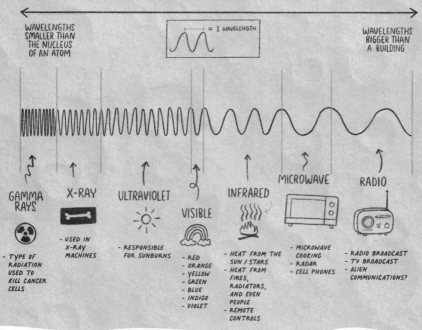

WAVELENGTHS SMALLER THAN THE NUCLEUS OF AN ATOM

= 1 WAVELENGTH

WAVELENGTHS BIGGER THAN A BUILDING

GAMMA RAYS
- TYPE OF RADIATION USED TO KILL CANCER CELLS

X-RAY
- USED IN X-RAY MACHINES

ULTRAVIOLET
- RESPONSIBLE FOR SUNBURNS

VISIBLE
- RED
- ORANGE
- YELLOW
- GREEN
- BLUE
- INDIGO
- VIOLET

INFRARED
- HEAT FROM THE SUN / STARS
- HEAT FROM FIRES, RADIATORS, AND EVEN PEOPLE
- REMOTE CONTROLS

MICROWAVE
- MICROWAVE COOKING
- RADAR
- CELL PHONES

RADIO
- RADIO BROADCAST
- TV BROADCAST
- ALIEN COMMUNICATIONS?

The two men realized that their idea might be considered more science fiction than real science, but the last line of their paper sums up the reality of the situation:

> The probability of success is difficult to estimate; but if we never search the chance of success is zero.

BACK TO FRANK AND OZ

Remember Chapter 8? (You really should—it was only one chapter back.) That's when we learned about how Frank Drake dreamed up his famous equation after listening to two nearby stars, hoping to pick up radio waves from an advanced civilization. He'd called the endeavor Project Ozma after the princess of Oz (a setting that was first introduced in the novel *The Wonderful Wizard of Oz*).

Project Ozma operated from April to July 1960, during which Drake and his team listened to the skies for approximately 150 hours. The project mostly used existing instruments and cost only about $2,000—spending more on the hunt for aliens may have been considered frivolous. Drake focused on two close-ish stars, Tau Ceti and Epsilon Eridani; each is about eleven light-years away. He and his team searched for noticeable patterns among the static. Early on, they thought they'd made a discovery, but the noise came from a passing plane. In the end, they found nothing, but this is considered by many to be the first SETI study.

(It should be noted that Dr. Drake developed this search-for-radio-waves idea independently from the Cornell physicists who wrote the paper. Just shows that great minds think alike!)

While our eyes are limited in what we can see, engineers have created telescopes and other devices that can detect waves outside the visible range. As a matter of fact, most of what makes up the universe is invisible to our eyes! The James Webb telescope takes pictures of infrared space and then uses computers to create models we can physically see.

Note: Sound waves are not electromagnetic waves; they're mechanical waves and cannot travel in a vacuum (meaning: an area void of matter, even air).

LGM (LITTLE GREEN MEN)

Sixty years ago, not everyone with a telescope searched for alien life and alien signals, but it was probably never far from any astronomer's thoughts. With computers and other improving technology, the slow and tedious work of observing and analyzing the night sky was happening worldwide. In England in 1967, a young graduate student named Jocelyn Bell Burnell began working on a project with an astronomer at Cambridge University. The goal was to study quasars, which are bright lights found in the center of some galaxies. Bell Burnell, along with several others, helped design and build a radio telescope for the job, but when the telescope went into use, her colleagues left for other opportunities. Only Bell Burnell stayed to run the telescope.

At this time, the computer available for the program didn't have much memory. Instead of the data being saved on a disc or hard drive, it was printed out. Bell Burnell said she looked through about 900 feet (275 meters) of printouts daily. In the first six months, she discovered about 100 quasars. *Success!*

But something even more interesting also showed up on these papers. The first mysterious signal appeared on August 6, 1967. Bell Burnell noted it and moved on.

A few months later, a high-speed recording found more of these strange signals. They were radio pulses, repeating a little more than a second apart at precise intervals—like a clock keeping perfect time. Her advisor, the head of the program, labeled the find LGM-1 for Little Green Men because he believed the signal had to be artificial—created by something or someone. Bell Burnell disagreed and found more of these curious, perfectly timed radio pulses. Later, these blinky objects would be identified as pulsars, which are spinning neutron stars (meaning: a dead star that's 12 miles [20 kilometers] across and the densest object known in the universe). In 1968, Bell Burnell and her professor published a paper about their findings. And in 1974, that professor and another colleague received the Nobel Prize in Physics for the discovery. Bell Burnell did not. *(This is unfair, and it sucks, right? There is a long history of sexism and racism in science, academics, and many industries. For example, only white men have walked on the Moon. We'd like to think this would not happen today.)*

Still, Bell Burnell's discovery had—and still has—a remarkable impact on astronomy. Because they're so precise, pulsars can be used to make all sorts of calculations in space: measure distances, calculate weights, find centers of gravity, and more.

WOW!

On August 15, 1977, the Big Ear telescope (my favorite name of a telescope ever) at Ohio State University recorded an interesting signal. It lasted seventy-two seconds, and the radio wave frequency was in the range scientists believed was ideal for interstellar communication. Big Ear was working—listening and collecting data—even while the scientists were resting, so when the telescope discovered the signal, there was no human nearby eavesdropping with giant 1977-style headphones. It would be days before SETI scientist Jerry Ehman would review the data on paper printouts. The pages contained a series of low numbers, 1s, 2s, 3s, and 4s, which was normal. These digits represented ordinary background noises of the night sky. But then the telescope had picked up something quite unusual. The signal got *noisier*, so noisy that the scale went from digits to letters. (The computer could spit out only single characters; after 7, 8, and 9 came A, B, C, D, and so on.) Ehman used a red pen to circle a column with 6, E, Q, U, J, 5. For perspective, the U signal is thirty times higher than ordinary background noises. And he wrote "Wow!" in the margin. This brief reading became known as the Wow! signal.

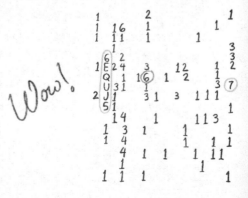

The signal did not repeat. The widely held belief is that a signal meant to be heard in far-off solar systems should be repeated. (You can imagine a person in an old movie shouting into a walkie-talkie, "Mayday! Mayday! Mayday!" Repeating yourself gets attention.) Without duplicate data, scientists could not pinpoint the exact location of the sound. For decades, astronomers have continued to search for the Wow! signal. They've been unsuccessful.

Forty years later, one astronomer developed a theory to explain the mysterious noise. The hypothesis is that Comet 266P/Christensen caused the unusual reading. Comet 266P was in the right place, and a comet with a hydrogen cloud could have created the signal detected by Big Ear. The astronomer and his team recently observed Comet 266P (along with other comets) and got a similar reading, though not as strong. The signal could have been weaker because Comet 266P has lost some mass in the past forty years, or because the satellite used to capture the reading wasn't as large as Big Ear. The paper claims that the Wow! signal was from a comet, even if it wasn't specifically from Comet 266P.

Still, not everyone is convinced that the Wow! signal is natural—or caused by a comet. (One amateur astronomer and YouTuber did his own research and believes the signal may have come from an exoplanet.) Professional (and amateur) astronomers will continue to study the skies and the data, hoping to get to the bottom of this anomaly.

COULD ALIENS HEAR US?

Earthlings have been using radio waves to communicate for more than a century. A ground-based antenna might broadcast music for radio or programs for television. But some of these waves don't end up just on Earthly devices; they travel away from our planet and eventually into deep space. Yes! Early episodes of black-and-white TV shows are sailing through the Milky Way at light speed. A civilization of sophisticated aliens could tune in to *I Love Lucy*...or could they?

Radio waves degrade over long distances, and aliens would need to be close by and have ginormous telescopes to pick up our channels. Or, at the very least, they'd need technology better than our own. It is possible that someone is listening but not likely. Also, as Earthly communication improves, the signals we beam into the air are more efficient than they were decades ago, so we're leaking less into space. Our species is cosmically quieter.

However, there's an issue with all our through-the-air technology, like cell phones and Wi-Fi. It's making SETI scientists' jobs harder here on Earth. Some radio frequencies are so jammed with human-made signals that astronomers are forced to use different channels. The crowding can also lead to false finds. Researchers might think a signal came from deep space, but it was really from down the road. To help cut down on the interference, places like the Green Bank Observatory in West Virginia are "quiet zones." No cell service or Wi-Fi is allowed in a 13,000-square-mile (33,670-square-kilometer) area. (They also have restrictions on microwaves and Bluetooth technology. It must be like living in a different time!)

PROJECT BREAKTHROUGH LISTEN

In 2015, Israeli billionaire Yuri Milner and renowned theoretical physicist Stephen Hawking announced a new ten-year project called Breakthrough Listen. (Milner is an ultrarich guy who loves science and privately funds projects he's passionate about through his foundation, Breakthrough Initiatives.) The program will dish out $100 million in funding over a decade to the most promising SETI projects. A large portion of the money will go to renting observation time at key telescopes. Instead of building their own massive observatories, SETI projects borrow time at existing telescopes around the world, in places like Green Bank (Drake's original research hangout), Australia, South America, and New Mexico. Big chunks of change are also being funneled into computing. SETI projects collect lots and lots of data, and major computers are needed to sort through the information. (Thankfully, scientists no longer have to read through pages of printouts anymore! Trees are probably thankful too.)

According to the Breakthrough Listen website, the aim is to listen in on the 1 million stars nearest to Earth and to check out the 100 closest galaxies for incoming messages. The equipment the programs will have access to can pick up aircraft-like radar from the nearest star systems. (That means if those planets have something like air traffic control, SETI scientists might be able to detect those signals.)

The Breakthrough Listen project is well beyond its halfway point. And, as you probably guessed, the program has yet to find any alien civilizations. There have been "close calls" (like radio signals made by human tech) but not the results Milner and most of the world have hoped for. Still, Milner has hinted that he might fund the search beyond 2025.

SETI TOMORROW

When Dr. Drake ran his first SETI experiment over sixty years ago, he'd check one frequency at a time (imagine scanning through channels on a radio). Now SETI scientists can listen in on billions of frequencies at once. Much more efficient! In addition, some programs are firing up new hunting strategies that go beyond radio waves. Perhaps our intelligent alien friends don't want to send us messages by radio waves. Perhaps they think that technology is old-fashioned and out of style. Perhaps these extraterrestrials are into lasers! That's essentially the thinking behind OSETI (optical search for extraterrestrial intelligence). Instead of searching for radio waves, the goal is to find artificial light—like lasers, which are narrow, focused beams of light of the same wavelength.

One program that's currently operational is LaserSETI. The project has instruments monitoring the night sky over the Pacific Ocean in two locations—one on the Hawaiian island of Maui that watches the east, and one in Kenwood, California, that watches the west. This setup allows for overlap, which can help confirm or debunk a possible alien laser beam detection. The cameras in Hawai'i and California look for individual bright points of light in one color (a single wavelength) that don't fade in or out but instead turn on and off quickly. (Imagine a red laser pointer like the kind a teacher may use during a lesson but a gazillion times more powerful.) Since lasers do not occur in nature, spotting one would mean spotting alien technology.

Theoretically, a laser signal could come from anywhere in the universe, and another ambitious project has been proposed to capture the entire sky. The scientists behind PANOSETI (pulsed all-sky near-infrared optical SETI) hope to have hundreds of observatories across the globe. Each observatory would actually be a collection of eighty smaller telescopes arranged in a faceted-dome shape (imagine a bug's eye) and able to see in many directions. Unlike the radio telescopes, which search only a fraction of space at a time, PANOSETI will continuously watch the entire night skies for quick bursts of light or infrared radiation—we're talking super-quick, nanosecond-long flashes. And because of the strategic locations of the domes, astronomers would be able to rule out glitches and local Earthly light. Prototype telescopes have been installed at the Lick Observatory in California.

TECHNOSIGNATURES

Intelligent aliens are bound to have some cool toys and abilities, right? Technosignatures (meaning: evidence of current or past technology) include SETI favorites like radio waves and laser beams. Then there are also things like:

- Pollutants—industrial chemicals in an alien atmosphere might be detected with spectroscopes.
- Spacecraft—we'll save this for Chapter 10.
- Visible light—imagine a lit-up Earth at night; more powerful telescopes are needed.
- Megastructures—not skyscrapers, bridges, or great walls; think bigger!

One megastructure that might get noticed by our telescopic technology is the hypothetical Dyson sphere. (We Earthlings currently don't have the ability or resources to create such a structure, but advanced aliens might.) It's named in honor of theoretical physicist Freeman Dyson, who suggested that the energy needs of all tech-loving creatures will grow exponentially over time—a trait humans seem to exhibit. Dyson estimated that over 3,000 years, a civilization might need a trillion times more energy. To satisfy this hunger, the civilization would have to harness much of its star's power. This could be accomplished by building a ginormous solar-panel-like structure around the star—a Dyson sphere. From a great distance away, a star with a Dyson sphere would appear as just a star—a twinkly light—but if scientists compared optical data with infrared data, they could determine possible candidates. A star covered by a partial megastructure would have less visible light, but the warm Dyson sphere would have infrared waves. So far, no Dyson spheres have been located.

SETI, MEET METI

It's clear that the search for intelligent extraterrestrial life would be easier if a civilization continually beamed messages into space, like a lighthouse. And maybe that's precisely what *we* should be doing. Humans may not have the technology to travel across the galaxy (or even across our solar system), but we *can* send a "hello" message. That's the idea behind METI, or messaging extraterrestrial intelligence: Say hi and let the technologically superior beings reply or visit.

This idea of communicating with those beyond our planet is not new. In the 1800s, astronomer Joseph Johann von Littrow suggested creating massive trench fires in the

Sahara Desert in various shapes that far-out observers might see. That never happened. In the '60s, the Soviets used radio waves to send Morse code to Venus. They didn't get a reply. In 1974, Frank Drake, Carl Sagan, and other scientists sent an easily decodable radio message from the Arecibo Observatory in Puerto Rico to a star cluster about 25,000 light-years away. It included a picture of a stick figure, a diagram of DNA, a map of our solar system (including our location—third planet from the Sun), and additional rudimentary info about Earth and us. The message was sent about fifty years ago and will be en route to its destination for another 24,950 years.

Since the Arecibo message, many other dispatches have been sent into space. NASA has even sent physical gifts! Voyagers 1 and 2, both launched in 1977, carry the Golden Record—a literal golden phonographic record containing Earth's sounds and sights, including greetings in fifty-five languages. The message in Mandarin says: "Hope everyone's well. We are thinking about you all. Please come here to visit when you have time." The message in Rajasthani is less inviting: "Hello to everyone. We are happy here and you be happy there." Some METI activity is not science but simply a publicity stunt, like in 2018 when a Doritos commercial was sent to a star system forty-two light-years away. *(If aliens are there, do you think they'd prefer Cool Ranch or Nacho Cheese?)*

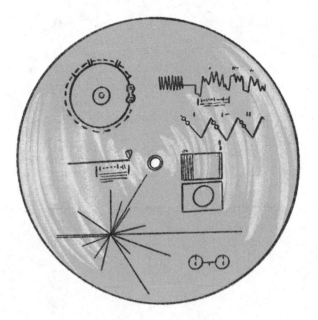

GOLDEN RECORD

A recent scientific paper introduced a new METI project called Beacon in the Galaxy (BITG). Like the Arecibo message, it would use a simple code to convey info about Earth, including math functions, male and female forms, common periodic elements, diagrams of DNA, directions to Earth, a map of Earth, and a please-write-back-soon request. The scientists would like to beam this message toward the galactic neighborhoods most likely to have life, areas not too far from the center of the galaxy. That's a minimum of 6,500 light-years away. Whether the BITG message gets sent this year or next, the reply is not happening in this lifetime.

SHOW ME THE MONEY

Searching for extraterrestrials takes some coin, and there's been a continued debate about who should pay the bill. Frank Drake's Project Ozma from 1960 was privately funded and cheap. He kept the cost to about $2,000 and used existing equipment. It wasn't until 1975 that NASA began some modest funding of SETI and, the following year, rolled the SETI branch of study into the Ames Research Center. But then, in 1978, Senator William Proxmire gave SETI his infamous Golden Fleece Award. (This is not a good thing. Proxmire liked to mock programs he didn't think the government should support financially.) All government funding was cut off in 1981. Temporarily. It was restored in 1983 when Carl Sagan convinced the senator that the SETI program was scientifically important. Things were okay for a decade, and then in 1992, the program got some excellent news. After NASA rebranded SETI to HRMS (High-Resolution Microwave Survey), Congress awarded the program $100 million to be paid out over ten years. *Wahoo!* But—you knew there was a "but"—a year later, Senator Richard Bryan stepped in and slashed the budget. Killed it! The HRMS program lost all federal funding again. Senator Bryan said, "This hopefully will be the end of Martian hunting season at the taxpayers' expense." Obviously, he wasn't paying close attention because SETI programs were not concerned with Mars.

Separately, the SETI Institute, which is behind many of the projects discussed in this chapter, was created as a nonprofit in 1984. It did receive some US government contracts through NASA for a time. After the money was cut off in the '90s, the institute survived on private funding, as it does today. (This includes the big bucks from Breakthrough Listen.)

The debate about who should pay SETI bills will likely continue indefinitely. Maybe even after intelligent extraterrestrial life is confirmed. However, this seems to be a golden age for SETI. A majority of the American public is on team Life Beyond Earth, which has helped move SETI work firmly into the "real science" category. More private money is being donated to research, and not just from billionaires. Crowdfunding is supporting many projects, with thousands of people contributing. Also, NASA, though not explicitly searching for aliens, continues to explore the Milky Way and the universe. (The agency is not just about training astronauts and sending them into space.) NASA's work, especially regarding exoplanets, is crucial to SETI scientists. For example, the JWST is *not* hunting for alien radio waves, but because it gathers vital information about distant stars and planets, SETI researchers can better target their own searches.

Of course, all this METI talk can't just be about technology and galactic location. There's a bigger question. Should we be telling the universe our address and other details? Some argue that we've already been accidentally broadcasting for over a century—we're talking about radio waves, radar, and other communications—so a direct message doesn't put us at any additional risk. Some warn that we're inviting trouble and can look to our own past of colonization. Then there's a question about the question. Who gets to decide whether we should try to contact extraterrestrials? Elected politicians, the United Nations, members of scientific panels, a survey of Earthlings? Searching for aliens and exploring space aren't just about answering tech questions. The ethical questions can be just as tricky.

MEET ASTRONOMER JILL TARTER

Credit: Seth Shostak

A legend! That's the simplest way to describe Dr. Jill Tarter. In 1965, she was the only woman in a class of 300 undergraduate engineers at Cornell University. When she went to Berkeley for graduate school, she was one of two women in the astronomy department. She faced sexist pushback from professors and classmates. After graduating, Tarter focused on the SETI side of astronomy. This was another kind of obstacle because not all scientists took the search for extraterrestrials seriously. But Tarter did. "Are we alone?" was not a philosophical question for her but a science question. She set out to find an answer using scientific methods.

Dr. Jill Tarter helped create the first SETI-type program at NASA (which eventually lost funding), and in 1984, she co-founded the non-profit SETI Institute. Tarter's career and passion for SETI also inspired the character Ellie Arroway in the movie *Contact* (which was originally a book written by Carl Sagan).

In 2012, Jill Tarter retired, but she remains passionate about SETI and astronomy. She continues to share her passion with colleagues and with students. She was kind enough to answer a few questions for us by email.

Q: Have you always been interested in space and the possibility of life beyond Earth? Did you have a favorite subject in school?

A: When I was about eight years old, I remember walking with my dad along the keys of the west coast of Florida and looking up and thinking that some creature up there was seeing our Sun in our sky and wondering who might live there. Math was my favorite subject.

Q: What new or in-the-works technology are you excited about? What could revolutionize the SETI field?

A: There are a number of Earth- and space-based telescopes on the near horizon that should open up large portions of observational parameter space. Using machine learning to help us recognize different kinds of signal patterns is really exciting.

Q: What are your thoughts on METI? Should Earthlings try to make contact?

A: We are too immature to take this on. We can barely finish a two-year plan; transmitting might have to continue for centuries or millennia until we overlap temporally with another technological civilization.

Q: Do you ever dream about the day humans confirm we're not alone? What do you imagine happening?

A: I think it will change everything in many ways we cannot predict.

Q: In this book, I tell readers they can be team Only Earth or team Life Beyond Earth. At this time, we can't prove either group right or wrong. Can we assume you are a Life Beyond Earth–er?

A: Yes, but of course nobody knows.

Q: Any advice for young readers who'd like to search for aliens in the future as a career?

A: Study math and find something you really like to do, get really good at it, and see how it might apply to searching for life beyond Earth.

CHAPTER 10

DUDE! WHAT WAS THAT?

UFOS AND UAPS

Receiving an ET message by radio waves or laser pulse would be incredible. But this whole search for aliens would be much easier if they visited Earth in person...or in alien. If we could capture these visitors on a cell phone camera, the video would go absolutely viral. But what if we didn't see the actual extraterrestrials, just their vehicles? It's possible they'd send drones or robots, just like NASA has sent to Mars. It would still be awesome, assuming the video wasn't a shaky, blurry mess.

Plenty of people claim to have spotted alien spacecraft or, more accurately, unidentified flying objects. Labeling these *objects* "spaceships," "spacecraft," or "flying saucers" is a bit too definitive. "UFO" works better because it's a category of unknowns—like how, for decades, US military pilots have encountered things they can't identify. As these sightings became more common, the government decided to investigate. It came up with a new name: unidentified aerial phenomenon, or UAP (because the abbreviation UFO sounds too much like it belongs in a comic book). And in 2021, the government issued a report on its findings.

WORTH INVESTIGATING?

You'd better believe it! The US government has investigated UFOs in the past. From 1947 to 1969, the Air Force ran a program called Project Blue Book. Of the over 12,000 UFO sightings it reviewed, only about 700 remain unexplained. Still, the project drew three major conclusions.

1. None of these sightings were ever a threat to national security.

2. None of the UFOs appeared more sophisticated than our modern technology.

3. No vehicles were extraterrestrial in nature.

It would be almost four decades before the government again looked into the unidentified. In 2007, the Advanced Aerospace Threat Identification Program (AATIP) secretly began at the Pentagon. The investigators were charged with looking into UAPs, especially those encountered by military pilots, including the November 2004 *Nimitz* encounter.

Off the coast of San Diego, California, crew members on the Navy cruiser USS *Princeton* repeatedly spotted an unknown aircraft that acted kinda weird. The mysterious vessel would suddenly appear on radar at 80,000 feet (24,000 meters) above the ocean, then drop crazy quick to 20,000 feet (6,100 meters) and hover there. Then it might disappear or shoot back up. *Weird, indeed.* The next time the strange object appeared, two Navy Super Hornet aircraft from the USS *Nimitz* were participating in a routine exercise nearby. The pilots got instructions to check it out! *What was this thing?*

At first, the two fighter pilots didn't see anything, even though the radio controller told them they were in the right spot. Then they looked down at the ocean and noticed an area where the sea was churning. One of the pilots said it looked like the water was boiling. Above the frothy water was a white aircraft that resembled a 40-foot-long (12-meter-long) Tic Tac. One of the planes moved in for a closer look. As the Super Hornet went down, the Tic Tac came up as if the two had planned to meet in the middle. When the Super Hornet tried to approach directly, the Tic Tac sped away like nothing the pilot had ever seen before. It didn't appear to have wings or rotors or any means of propulsion. A few minutes later, the UAP was picked up on radar 60 miles (97 kilometers) away. It had moved *really* far, *really* fast.

Another jet was sent out to track the mysterious craft. It captured seventy-six seconds of video with a targeting camera, which was declassified and shared with the public years later. One of the Super Hornet pilots admitted that he probably would not have said anything about the Tic Tac if he'd been alone that day. It was just too unbelievable. The object in question has still not been identified.

While the AATIP was officially defunded in 2012, the program carried on in other forms, and the government kept tabs on sightings. In 2017, three videos were leaked to the *New York Times*, including the footage from the *Nimitz* encounter (also called the Tic Tac encounter). One of the other videos (which is actually two recordings together) was filmed from Jacksonville, Florida, in 2015. It's just over a minute long and includes conversations between US Navy crew members.

Here's some of the dialogue:
(First video)

This is a *[swear word]* drone, bro.

There's a whole fleet of them.

My gosh.

Look at that thing, dude.

Look at that thing.

It's rotating.

(Second video)

What the *[swear word]* is that thing?

Oh my gosh, dude.

Wow. What is that?

Look at it fly. Ha. Ha.

While an extraterrestrial visitor is the least likely explanation for the sighting, the Navy crew members on the video seem obviously excited and bewildered. So what was it?

THE OFFICIAL FINDINGS OF THE UNITED STATES GOVERNMENT

On June 25, 2021, the Office of the Director of National Intelligence released a report with the somewhat dull title *Preliminary Assessment: Unidentified Aerial Phenomena*. A better heading would have been *Our First Findings on UFOs*. (But, as we know, the government prefers "UAP" to "UFO.") The paper was made available on a Friday night in summer, and many wondered whether the government did this to avoid attention. If so, it didn't work. Plenty of newspapers, magazines, TV news programs, and people on the internet noticed. So what did the report say?

Basically, it's inconclusive!

This report reviewed UAP sightings from 2004 to 2021, with most of the objects having been observed with multiple sensors, meaning not just seen but also detected on things like radar and infrared imaging. The report's favorite UAP data came from the USG (US government), primarily the military and FBI. Of the 144 UAPs from the USG—are you tired of abbreviations yet?—eighteen appeared "to demonstrate advanced technology." Basically, the report admits that these objects were operating in a way that seems beyond our current capabilities. They moved too fast or turned too quickly, or hovered in place in windy situations. Definite head-scratchers.

The report never uses the words "extraterrestrial," "alien," or "outer space." Instead, the investigators came up with five categories—or five possibilities.

Airborne Clutter: Normal stuff we expect to find in the air, like birds, drones (which the report calls recreational uncrewed aerial vehicles, or UAVs), balloons, and plastic bags. While not explicitly mentioned, we could also add runaway kites, very well-thrown Frisbees, Iron Man, and dogs with jet packs.

Natural Atmospheric Phenomena: Moisture, ice, and hot or cold air pockets could interfere with radar and infrared systems. Basically, the weather could be messing with our technology.

USG or Industry Developmental Programs: Some UAPs could be objects created by a top-secret US government program. But the report is the result of a (once) top-secret program, and the investigators seem confident they would know whether the group down the hall built these UAPs. No "Made in the USA" sticker here.

Foreign Adversary Systems: But maybe some unexplained thingamajigs are Russian or Chinese tech. Other nations might have better toys than the USA. Foreign governments or companies operating abroad could be behind the UAPs in this category.

Other: The report admits that not all UAPs fit nicely into the above four categories. These could be something else. (I always hated when a question on a multiple-choice test had an "other" option. It would make me doubt everything listed above it!) The objects that "display unusual flight characteristics" can't be birds, clouds, or advanced tech by aggressive governments. The UAPTF (Unidentified Ariel Phenomena Task Force) needs more information on these "others." It's safe to say that we all want it!

Of the 144 UAPs, the report cleared up just one. The investigators determined "with high confidence" that it was a deflating balloon. We may never know what's behind the rest of the UAPs. The nine-page report admitted that UAPs pose a danger to pilots and possibly to national security. The UAPTF wants all unknown objects to be documented. In the past, reporting a UFO sighting would likely hurt a service member's career—or at least get them made fun of in the mess hall. Now the Navy and Air Force have formal ways to report these events. Maybe someday we'll get the information we need. Decades ago, Carl Sagan popularized the following expression:

> Extraordinary claims require extraordinary evidence.

(Or ECREE, if you want an acronym and another idea for a nerdy tattoo—or T-shirt.) These UAPs are interesting but not extraordinary evidence. We'll have to live with inconclusive results. At least for now.

DUDE, WHAT WAS THAT? SOLAR SYSTEM EDITION

Sadly, it's unlikely that any of the UAPs are extraterrestrial. We don't know for sure (think of that Other category!), but Earthly explanations make more sense: equipment malfunctions, known tech, natural phenomena, and so on. But one time, an object from deep space *did* visit our solar system. (Actually, it's happened more than once, but this first occurrence got the most attention.)

On October 19, 2017, astronomers in Hawai'i, who were hunting for potential Earth-bound killer asteroids, noticed something unusual through their megatelescope. It was an object traveling 50 miles (80 kilometers) per second away from the Sun. When the astronomers calculated the trajectory of this mystery object, they realized it came from outside our solar system. *Whoa!* It was given a formal name, 1I/2017 U1, but soon after, it would be called 'Oumuamua, which is

Hawaiian for "a messenger from afar arriving first." *A perfect name!*

Right away, astronomers worldwide pointed their telescopes toward the speedy mystery. Scientists had to act fast because 'Oumuamua would not be sticking around.

Here's what they learned about the visitor!

- Cigar-shaped, which is unlike anything ever discovered
- Ten times longer than it is wide. Estimates put it at a quarter mile (400 meters) long.
- Rotates on its axis every 7.3 hours
- Brightness changes by a factor of ten as it spins, which is also unlike anything ever discovered
- Dense, likely made of rock and metal, with no water or ice
- Reddish
- Speedy and getting speedier (the object accelerated)

Unfortunately, 'Oumuamua wasn't yet known when it was closest to Earth on October 14, which means scientists could not capture photographs. Optical telescopes focused on the right area of the sky would have been required. (And 'Oumuamua is not something a Navy pilot would have seen. It stayed in space.) Our planet was already in its rearview mirror when the Hawaiian astronomers told the world about it, and by February, it was too distant for any telescope to observe.

So what was it exactly? While 'Oumuamua acted like a comet—specifically, speeding up after passing the Sun, which is very comet-like—it was missing a key comet feature: a tail! Typically, the Sun's heat vaporizes a portion of an icy comet, creating a tail of dust and gas. 'Oumuamua was tailless. Some scientists categorize it as an asteroid, but its brightness, shape, and acceleration are oddball-ish for asteroids. Simply labeling it an "interstellar object" seems to be less objectionable.

A few astronomers think 'Oumuamua might be something more interesting. The former longtime chair of Harvard's department of astronomy, Avi Loeb, believes 'Oumuamua might be our first encounter with extraterrestrial technology.

Reasons why it might be alien tech:

- **Shape:** While 'Oumuamua is often described as cigar-shaped, it might be more pancake-shaped. In our solar system, we haven't seen anything similar. The wide, thin body could be ideal for absorbing light and using it for energy—similar to a solar sail or lightsail. (More on lightsails in Chapter 12.)

- **Brightness**: Our Sun gives off light, and the planets, moons, asteroids, and so on reflect light. Because 'Oumuamua was tumbling through space, it sometimes reflected less light and sometimes more—sometimes as much as ten times more. This is also something not seen in our solar system. Perhaps it's constructed of artificial materials and not natural.

- **Acceleration:** It's not a comet, but it's accelerating. Why? It could be using our Sun's light to push itself through space, again similar to solar sails.

- **Age:** 'Oumuamua's age is unknown, but because of the distance it's had to travel (though we also don't know exactly where it came from), it has to be at least hundreds of millions of years old. According to Loeb, it could be an ancient alien artifact—and not operational anymore. Space junk. As mentioned in previous chapters, our own Voyager spacecraft have left our solar system, and they may approach another star in 40,000 years. At that time, they'll be out of battery and might appear to be asteroids or comets.

 Many astronomers and astrobiologists disagree with the idea that 'Oumuamua is ancient alien technology. While the object behaved oddly, it's not beyond explanation. A recent paper suggests that it could be a fragment of a Pluto-like exoplanet made of primarily frozen nitrogen—a nitrogen iceberg, if you will. This theory accounts for the shape, color, brightness, and speed.

Then, in 2019, astronomers found their first interstellar comet, which was named 2I/Borisov. Unlike 'Oumuamua, this object acted and looked like a comet. Following this, a 2021 report from the Initiative for Interstellar Studies suggested that our solar system might get as many as seven interstellar visitors a year. These objects are likely to follow predictable orbits, which might give scientists and engineers a chance to meet up with one. (NASA has sent probes to *local* asteroids in the past.) This might be the easiest way to learn about the environment beyond our solar system—even if the object isn't an ancient alien artifact.

While the government and scientists are not keen on using the term UFO, there are plenty of objects that fit this category. Maybe someday we'll change the *U* to an *E* for EFO—an extraterrestrial flying object. That would certainly make Life Beyond Earth–ers happy.

CHAPTER 11

ARE ALIEN ENCOUNTER STORIES REAL?

NOPE!

Let's all admit it: Firsthand accounts of alien encounters are fascinating. If I sat next to a woman on a plane and she asked if I wanted to hear the story of the time she met an alien, I'd scream, "Yes, please!" And yet, if the woman on my other side asked if I wanted to hear about her job at NASA searching for biosignatures, I'd also scream, "Yes, please!" I don't know who I'd like to listen to first. Don't make me pick. I just hope it's a long plane ride.

Of course, it would be much easier to believe the scientist. She'd be professionally required to document, duplicate, and verify her findings. My other new best friend just needs to be entertaining.

Let's look at some of the most captivating and popular stories to emerge over the past few decades. Spoiler alert:

None of these are real evidence of extraterrestrial contact. *Bummer!* Therefore, these tales are unlikely to persuade Only Earth–ers to switch teams and will also not help Life Beyond Earth–ers win any arguments.

ROSWELL

In June 1947, a rancher named W. W. "Mac" Brazel found something unusual on his property about 80 miles (130 kilometers) from Roswell, New Mexico. An object had crashed. He later described the site as "a large area of bright wreckage made up of rubber strips, tinfoil, a rather tough paper, and sticks." He didn't know what it was or where it came from. Mac collected the debris and took it to the sheriff in Roswell. The sheriff was also perplexed, so he called a colonel at the Roswell Army Air Field (RAAF). The colonel was similarly baffled, so he shared the find with his superiors. An intelligence officer from RAAF made a statement about the mysterious debris, and on July 8, the *Roswell Daily Record* ran a front-page story with this headline:

RAAF CAPTURES FLYING SAUCER ON RANCH IN ROSWELL REGION

Even without the internet, that story went viral. At least for a day…

Almost immediately, other military authorities said the

crashed flying saucer was actually a *crashed* weather balloon—*crashing* the hopes of those wanting to find aliens. The paper ran a new story:

ARMY DEBUNKS ROSWELL FLYING DISK AS WORLD SIMMERS WITH EXCITEMENT

But Roswell wasn't the only location with reports of mysterious happenings. Around the same time, a Navy seaman saw six UFOs near Puget Sound in Washington State. He shared his story, and the next day, "men in black" spoke to him about the incident. (In pop culture and in conspiracy lore, men in black are anonymous government officials who investigate—and cover up!—reports of aliens and UFOs.) Not long after, a pilot saw nine UFOs near Mount Rainier, also in Washington. *What was happening?* That's just too many coincidences. The US Army must have been lying about the weather balloon!

Yes, the US Army was lying. But sadly, it wasn't hiding aliens or flying saucers. The wreckage was from Project Mogul—a top-secret spying endeavor meant to keep tabs on the USSR. The US government used balloons with sensitive microphones to record sound waves from the Soviet nuclear bomb test. A full report wasn't released to the public until 1997.

By most accounts, Roswell, New Mexico, has embraced its

alien past. The city's logo is an *R* with a flying saucer cut-out in the center. Visitors can explore the International UFO Museum and Research Center, the UFO Spacewalk and Gallery, and Spaceport Roswell, a virtual reality experience of 1947 Roswell. The local businesses are also far-out, including the famous UFO-shaped McDonald's and a Dunkin'/Baskin-Robbins with a 20-foot-tall (6-meter-tall) big-eyed alien out front.

AREA 51

Area 51 is the "top-secret" US Air Force base located in Nevada, about 120 miles (195 kilometers) north of Las Vegas. But if you look to Google Maps for directions, you'll get this reply: *Sorry, we could not calculate directions from "Las Vegas, Nevada" to "Area 51, Nevada."* Proof the government is hiding something? Nope! Just proof that it doesn't want visitors—human or other.

Actually, the famed Area 51 is only a portion of the massive 2.9 million–acre (11,740-square-kilometer) Nevada Test and Training Range (NTTR), which is almost twice the size of Delaware. Before the 1950s, the United States tested nuclear weapons in this isolated desert location. When the government went looking for a place to develop new top-secret technology, this seemed like a perfect spot. (Who would go snooping around a nuclear testing facility? No one! And don't believe the comic books about radiation turning people into superheroes. The stuff is deadly!)

What new technology was the government trying to keep quiet? Mostly awesome new aircraft. This was the 1950s, during the Cold War and before military satellites but after the spy balloons of Project Mogul. The United States government wanted to know what the USSR was up to and was especially interested in Soviet nuclear technology and missile capabilities. The US Air Force needed a plane that could go really far (all the way to the USSR), go really high (so it wouldn't be detected), and go really fast (so it wouldn't be captured or shot down). The result was the U-2. These planes and their pilots did important spy work for years. But once they were discovered by the Soviets in 1960—a plane *was* shot down—the US military needed an even faster, higher, longer-flying aircraft. This result was the SR-71 Blackbird, and its testing began in 1964.

Of course, the Air Force couldn't tell the public about these training missions and secret planes. Then the Soviets would have known, and the Chinese, and the Koreans, and the Vietnamese—basically anyone the government was spying on at that time. But some secrets are harder to keep than others. Airline pilots and air traffic controllers noticed vehicles flying higher and faster than they thought possible. Rumors started. The alien mythology also got a boost from some of the CIA's practices surrounding Area 51. For example, personnel came and went by plane, which is not how most people get to work, and to maintain secrecy, the U-2 aircraft would arrive disassembled like a box of Legos and have to be put together. In UFO lore, flying saucers turn up at secret government agencies in pieces (perhaps because of a crash landing), and then the parts are studied and reassembled. At the very least, the people at Area 51 were acting all sneaky and making the neighbors paranoid.

Also, the CIA did not try to squash any of the alien and UFO rumors. The cloak of extraterrestrials was a good cover for the government's top-secret projects! Like if we were building a secret fort in the backyard that we didn't want our little brother to know about, we wouldn't argue with our adults if they said, "They're just tidying up the shed." Our little brother wouldn't be interested in a cleaning project. It's like that for the US government, except instead of chores, it's about aliens.

A WITNESS

Unidentified flying objects can be cause for excitement (and skepticism). Remember the *look at that thing, dude* moment with Navy crew members? Someone claiming to have seen alien bodies in a government facility is another level of wowzers (and cause for a truckload of skepticism). In May 1989, a "witness" named Robert Lazar spoke live to a Nevada TV station about his employment at Area 51. He claimed to have witnessed alien autopsies there. *What!* He said he worked in the S-4 section, which was where scientists— according to Lazar—analyzed alien spacecraft. Specifically, he was responsible for analyzing "element 115," an alien fuel. He even hinted that he may have taken some element 115 home with him, the way I might take extra napkins from a sandwich shop. Lazar also bragged to the world about his impressive science education from Caltech and MIT, yet there are no records of this. (Lazar insists the government destroyed them. *One of many cover-ups?*) Further investigation failed to find any hard evidence that he ever worked at Area 51.

But the alleged cover-ups don't stop there. In the late '90s, Lazar opened a business called United Nuclear, which sells some dangerous science stuff, like radioactive ore and ingredients for fireworks. Over the years, the company and Lazar had trouble with law enforcement for illegal sales, and the headquarters moved around. Then, in 2017, while a film crew was working on a documentary about Area 51, the authorities raided United Nuclear! According to documents filed with the Michigan police, the authorities wanted receipts, emails, and other paperwork related to the sale of thallium—a hard-to-come-by poison. A woman had been murdered with the stuff, and the FBI was trying to trace where it came from. (Lazar was not a suspect in the woman's death, but his company may have sold thallium to the killer.) Lazar and the film crew claimed that the search was just another government cover-up. His theory: The FBI had raided United Nuclear looking for element 115.

To some UFO enthusiasts, Lazar is a hero. For years, he's been sticking by his story even when the CIA, and FBI, and [insert any government agency name here] have tried to silence him. At one time, he claimed that the government shot out his tires. To other UFO believers, Lazar is an embarrassment, a joke, and he hurts their cause of getting to the bottom of UFO cases. When a reporter recently asked Lazar to reveal element 115, Lazar said he'd never do that. The public can decide whether to believe him or not, but Lazar will not be offering any proof.

ALIEN ABDUCTIONS

Reading stories about alleged alien abductions can be time-consuming and distracting—speaking from personal experience. There's no evidence or reason to believe any of these stories are true, but that doesn't mean they're not incredibly captivating. One of the first far-reaching alien abduction stories in the US was the tale told by Betty and Barney Hill, a middle-class couple from New England. She was a social worker, and he worked for the post office. Before the events of September 19, 1961, the couple didn't have any strong feelings about aliens or UFOs. That changed as they drove home from a trip late at night through the White Mountains of New Hampshire.

The couple spotted a light in the sky that didn't behave as expected. It hovered and grew brighter. They pulled over, exited the car, and looked at the strange object with binoculars. It appeared to be disc-shaped and had blinking lights. *A UFO!* (It certainly *was* something they could not identify!) Barney and Betty returned to their vehicle and continued down the highway. They stopped a second time when the UFO hovered right in front of them. Once again, Barney grabbed his binoculars, and this time, he spotted ten aliens with gray skin, big eyes, and dark uniforms. *What?!?!* He sensed trouble, and the Hills tried to get away. But there was a beeping sound coming from the trunk. An unknown force made them turn sharply and stop. The next thing they knew, it was two hours later, and they were 35 miles (56 kilometers) down the road. *What had happened?* The couple couldn't remember.

When they arrived home at sunrise, they noticed other strange details: There were shiny circular spots on their car's trunk, Betty's dress had tears and stains, Barney's shoes were scuffed, the binoculars strap was broken, and both their watches had stopped. Soon after, they reported the incident to officials at a US Air Force base. Afraid of being labeled crazy, they didn't share *all* the details.

Betty and Barney were not looking to become famous. They didn't tell the media. But Betty did want to know what had happened. She checked out books about flying saucers from the library and contacted a UFO expert. The couple felt they had found someone who would listen and not judge them. They shared all the details they could recall. After the discussions, Betty began having nightmares and remembering those missing hours of the incident. Then Betty and Barney sought a doctor who specialized in hypnotism for the anxiety caused by the ordeal. They also used hypnosis to recall more of their missing memories. Over months, Betty filled in the gaps in the story.

The Hills' ordeal didn't make the newspapers until 1963. Betty and Barney shared their account with a UFO study group. A reporter heard about it and published a column, and then the story went the 1960s version of viral. Betty and Barney's abduction captured people's imaginations across the US and the world. Their account influenced movies and books. But was it true? No, probably not.

Betty and Barney Hill certainly believed the story they eventually shared with the world. But much of what Betty recalled about that night came *after* reading books and talking to UFO experts, which may have influenced her memory. She also pieced together large chunks of the story from dreams or while under hypnosis. In the '60s, hypnosis was a newly popular practice and considered a legitimate way to uncover lost or suppressed memories. Neurologists now know more about the brain and do not think hypnosis is a reliable way to recall events. Simply put, our brains are not computers with millions of unlabeled .mov files that we can open if given the correct link. Brains are messy, emotional, imperfect, amazing organs that can be manipulated accidentally and on purpose. What really happened on the night of September 19, 1961, will likely never be known.

CROP CIRCLES, AKA ALIEN STREET SIGNS

I remember watching a television program as a kid about these strange patterns that appeared overnight in grain fields. Some were huge. Some were elaborate. Some were beautiful. All were a mystery—for a while. Most happened in Great Britain, but the circles were also found in other countries. The crops were not chemically altered or burned or destroyed, and some of the designs seemed too large and sophisticated to have been made by humans. While the first modern crop circle appeared in 1976, some historians suggest that the crop-circle phenomenon may be hundreds of years old based on ancient drawings. But where did they come from?

One theory is that crop circles were created by extraterrestrials, perhaps as a communication method—not necessarily to talk to us but rather to direct other aliens flying past, the way hikers might mark a trail. Or maybe aliens just like to doodle on planets they visit, like graffiti on a bridge or even a product logo—an alien Nike swoosh. For over a decade, the guessing game continued, going beyond aliens into both natural and paranormal realms (demons, witches, fairies, etc.).

However, a lot of the fun and mystery ended in 1991 when two Brits claimed they started creating crop circles thirteen years previous as a hoax. To make their designs, they needed only planks of wood (to smoosh down the crops) and rope (to pull the planks and create the mostly circular arrangements). Of course, the pair could not be responsible for crop circles worldwide, and some designs are much more intricate than a pattern of circles. It's believed other humans (not aliens or witches) are creating these crop circles as well, and they continue to this day. Modern-day creators might use drones and other devices to achieve the desired artwork. Still, some "croppies" believe that a portion of crop circles are real (not created by humans) because the designs in the fields are just too complicated for mere *Homo sapiens*—a species that's landed on the Moon only, like, six times. According to these believers, crop circles definitely have to be the work of creatures that have mastered intergalactic space travel.

Alien encounter stories and major government cover-ups will always be part of extraterrestrial lore. They make great tales and are better suited for the big screen than as evidence in the search for extraterrestrial intelligence. Only Earth–ers, of course, will not believe any UFO or ET story. And Life Beyond Earth–ers do not need to buy into these myths either.

CHAPTER 12

WHAT DOES THE FUTURE HOLD?

STUFF TO LOOK FORWARD TO

So, let's review where our search for aliens has taken us:

✓ We started with our man Fermi and his paradox: The Milky Way is teeming with stars and planets, so "Where is everybody?" *Sorry, Fermi, we still don't have an answer.*

✓ Missions across our solar system haven't given us any evidence of current or past life.

✓ Thousands of exoplanets have been discovered, but much is still unknown about most of these worlds.

✓ SETI scientists have listened to the skies for over half a century and heard nothing.

✓ Math can be used to illustrate the vastness and loneliness of the universe.

✓ And while not every UFO or UAP can be explained (yet!), there's no reason to believe they are from other worlds. Where does that leave us? The answer is obvious. We need to keep exploring.

Luckily, we learn more about our solar system, galaxy, and universe each year. We're living in a new space age when exploration beyond our world is exciting and supported by many in the public. We see this when our elected officials increase NASA's budget and when other countries and regions grow their own space agencies. Then you have the billionaires backing their pet projects. In Chapter 6, we looked at Earthlings' intentions with Mars, but what else is in the works? What projects might give us the answer to our title question—where are the aliens?—once and for all?

PROJECTS IN THE WORKS

JAMES WEBB SPACE TELESCOPE (JWST)

The JWST launched on December 25, 2021, and for the next decade, it will collect data for thousands of astronomers and hundreds of institutions. Unlike past satellites—Hubble, for example—the JWST will not orbit Earth; it will orbit the Sun. (However, it will stay in line with Earth.) The satellite has eighteen lightweight mirrors and a tennis-court-sized sun shield.

With the JWST, we will see farther into the universe than ever before—including back in time. (Fun fact: Sunlight takes eight minutes to reach Earth. So when you see the sunrise, you're actually watching history, what has already happened really far away.) The JWST will "look" 13.5 billion years into the past using infrared technology. The satellite will also

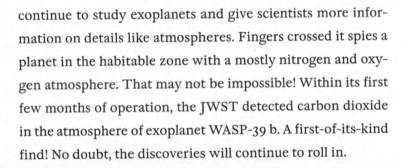

EARTH   JAMES
WEBB
SPACE
TELESCOPE

continue to study exoplanets and give scientists more information on details like atmospheres. Fingers crossed it spies a planet in the habitable zone with a mostly nitrogen and oxygen atmosphere. That may not be impossible! Within its first few months of operation, the JWST detected carbon dioxide in the atmosphere of exoplanet WASP-39 b. A first-of-its-kind find! No doubt, the discoveries will continue to roll in.

Fun Facts:

- Group project! This is a collaboration between NASA, ESA, CSA (Canadian Space Agency), and private companies.
- Initially, it was called the Next Generation Space Telescope.
- Slow going: The JWST needed a month to reach its destination, and once in orbit, it required an additional six months to become fully operational.

THE HUBBUB OVER HUBBLE

Space telescopes seem all the rage today, but that hasn't always been the case. The first sophisticated optical observatory sent to orbit Earth was the Hubble Space Telescope (HST). It launched aboard the Discovery space shuttle in April 1990, but the concept had been brewing since 1962—at which time it had a boring name, the Large Space Telescope. Most astronomers agreed that to get the best pictures of the stars, a telescope beyond Earth's atmosphere was necessary. (As we know, all those pesky gases in our atmosphere make stars twinkle and the night sky blurry.) Many people had to be convinced, from scientists to politicians, and the program finally got its funding in 1977.

In good news, the launch went well, and Hubble was released from Discovery by a robotic arm as planned. Within a month, NASA shared the first pictures captured by Hubble. But within two months, astronomers knew there was a major problem! One of Hubble's mirrors was defective—it had been made wrong. This was a bad look for NASA. It was called a tragedy and "a grim day for astronomy." The problem would eventually be fixed in December 1993 with a series of five spacewalks.

Hubble images and discoveries would inspire and influence astronomy for decades. Initially, it was designed to operate for only fifteen years, but it's still going—thanks to additional visits over time. And while the two telescopes are often compared, Webb is not intended to replace Hubble. There are no current plans to retire the HST.

Fun Facts:

- The HST is about the length of a school bus, 43.5 feet (13.2 meters) long. But no students (or any humans) are on board.

- Data from Hubble has been used in over 19,000 scientific papers. Lots of scientists are getting lots of use out of this piece of equipment.

- The satellite discovered two of the moons orbiting Pluto—Hydra and Nix.

- *Happy 13.8 billionth birthday, universe!* Hubble helped scientists establish the age of our universe.

- Hubble pictures are all in black and white. Scientists then use computer filters to put visible color on the images to highlight the different wavelengths from ultraviolet to infrared.

JUPITER ICY MOONS EXPLORER (JUICE)

What a great name for a mission! *Don't ya think?* This explorer will take a closer look at Jupiter and three of its moons, Ganymede, Callisto, and Europa (exciting places, according to Chapter 5). It's an ESA project searching for habitable areas on Jovian moons and checking out Jupiter's atmosphere. It's a tricky mission because Jupiter has quite the magnetosphere, which could mess with the sensitive equipment on board. JUICE won't land on any moons—all observations will be done from orbit.

Fun Facts:

- Quite a ride! The journey to Jupiter will take over seven and a half years.

- Deep enough? Aboard JUICE is the Radar for Icy Moons Exploration (RIME), equipment that will use radar to "look" over five miles (eight kilometers) deep into the ice. This is not deep enough to study subsurface oceans, but it will still offer valuable new information to scientists.

- Jupiter adventures for all! NASA will head back to the Jovian neighborhood with the launch of its Europa Clipper. China plans to send an orbiter to Callisto, making Jupiter and its moons one of the most visited areas in our solar system. (Mars, of course, wins that competition.)

DRAGONFLY MISSION (NOT ALL SPACE PROJECTS NEED ACRONYMS)

Jupiter's moons aren't the only ones getting visitors. NASA will send a rotorcraft to Saturn's moon Titan to study and collect samples from various locations across the surface. While this moon is cold (like, -290°F, or -179°C), it does have complex chemistry and underground water oceans. As we know, these are some of the life-building elements scientists seek. Dragonfly will land on Titan and then take short, thirty-minute flights, covering about 10 miles (16 kilometers) and collecting information at each stop. Because it's so far from Earth and its engineers, Dragonfly will have to operate autonomously (meaning: on its own).

Fun Facts:

- DragonCam! That's the name of the camera system that will be on board to take pics.

- The current schedule has Dragonfly leaving Earth in 2027 and arriving on Titan in 2034.

- This mission will operate for thirty-two months, and astrobiologists hope to find the building blocks of life or evidence of simple life. Unsurprisingly at this point in the book, no one expects intelligent aliens.

LUVEX (OFFICIAL NAME PENDING)

Every decade, the National Academies of Sciences, Engineering, and Medicine publish a guide that sets goals and encourages funding for the field of astronomy. The 2000 version gave strong support for the JWST. *Nice work!* (But let's think about timing for a moment. That program was initiated in 1996, got the top recommendation in 2000, and didn't launch until the last week of 2021. Astronomers and scientists really have to think long term.) The seventh and newest edition of the guide is officially titled *Pathways to Discovery in Astronomy and Astrophysics for the 2020s*, but is more lovingly called Astro2020.

What did Astro2020 endorse? This headline from *Scientific American* sums it up nicely:

HUNT FOR ALIEN LIFE TOPS NEXT-GEN WISH LIST FOR U.S. ASTRONOMY

For decades, the search for extraterrestrials often induced giggles or shame (especially from the US Congress budget committees). Now it seems we all want to know what—or *who*—is out there. (Except maybe Only Earth–ers. They may say it's a waste of time.)

One of the projects getting some *love* doesn't even have a name yet, just a nickname. LuvEx is actually the *marriage* of two proposals—LUVOIR (Large Ultraviolet Optical Infrared Surveyor) and HabEx (Habitable Exoplanet Observatory). Insiders report that LUVOIR is too ambitious and HabEx isn't ambitious enough; the ideal project is a combination of the two. Ultimately, we're looking at a new mega space telescope that would be three times larger than Hubble and observe exoplanets through direct imaging. *Pictures of exoplanets! The dream we all dream of!* Don't expect anything like the famous *Blue Marble* picture of Earth from the Apollo 17 mission. These pics are likely to be fuzzy dots, but they'll still be impressive, one-of-a-kind shots. LuvEx will use a starshade—a shield flying in front of the telescope, blocking out light. (It works kinda like a sun visor in a car.) This new technology should allow the discovery of planets that are 10 billion times fainter than their stars. Like Hubble, LuvEx will detect optical, infrared, and ultraviolet waves; it will also gather information about exoplanets' atmospheres and makeup.

Fun Facts:

- Seeing clearly: The 170-foot-wide (52-meter-wide), sunflower-shaped starshade will travel approximately 46,600 miles (75,000 kilometers) in front of the telescope to block starlight.

- Cha-ching! Astro2020 estimates an $11 billion price tag for LuvEx, plus an extra $8 billion for additional features.

- More patience, my friend! We thought waiting for JUICE and Dragonfly was exhausting. LuvEx might launch in the mid-2040s.

BREAKTHROUGH STARSHOT

Remember billionaire Yuri Milner and his Breakthrough Listen project (see Chapter 9)? Milner's foundation has brought us another ambitious (and wacky and fun) idea called Breakthrough Starshot, and he's working with Avi Loeb, the man who believes 'Oumuamua might be ancient alien technology (see Chapter 10). This project would send nanoprobes ("nano" means tiny) to the Alpha Centauri star system to collect all sorts of data, including pictures. When Breakthrough Starshot was introduced to the world in April 2016, astronomers had yet to announce any exoplanets in the star system.

Talk about shooting for the stars! The exoplanet Proxima Centauri b wouldn't be reported until that August.

The Starshot mission will have to travel 4.2 light-years. Obviously, the lighter the vessel, the faster it can go, so the nanoprobes won't be carrying any fuel. Instead, the probes, which are called StarChips, will use lightsails to glide through space. Imagine a sail, like on a boat, but instead of wind to push the vehicle, it uses light. The highly reflective lightsails will weigh approximately one gram (about the weight of a raisin) and measure about 13 feet (4 meters) on each side (the size of a large living-room rug). Each StarChip will also weigh approximately one gram and be the size of a postage stamp. Though they're small, they'll be packed with equipment like cameras, batteries, and navigation and communication instruments. (This tech is still being developed.)

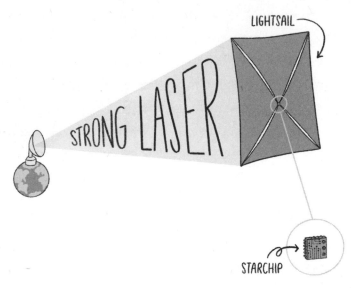

LIGHTSAIL

STRONG LASER

STARCHIP

The Starshot mission cannot launch directly from Earth because the components would burn up in the atmosphere. Instead, a mother ship will release the lightsails and nanoprobes from space. Then a strong laser (100 gigawatts or so) will be fired at the sails, giving them the jolt they'll need to travel at 20 percent the speed of light. That's fast, but it will still take some time for the nanoprobes to journey 4.2 light-years. We'll have to wait approximately twenty years before they reach the Alpha Centauri system and another four years for the first pictures and data to be beamed back to Earth. (The info being sent home can travel at light speed!) Also, the probes will not land or even slow down when they reach their destination. This is simply a flyby; the StarChips will snap pictures and collect data while traveling millions of miles per hour.

For any new scientific adventure, there are known obstacles that engineers must solve before the project is a go. For example, designing those StarChips, lightsails, the powerful laser, and the mother ship—just to name a few. The team also expects possible problems en route. These tiny probes are being launched into a hostile environment. Asteroids, comets, or even space dust could destroy them. Solar winds could push them off their path. But the team has a solution for this: send up lots and lots and lots of nanoprobes! Once they're designed and manufactured, it will be relatively cheap to launch thousands of them.

Another issue is signal strength. After the nanoprobes take pictures and collect data, they must send the information back to terrestrial scientists. Because of the StarChips' size and limited battery power, the signal will be weak. Big, sensitive instruments will be needed to listen for the nano-probes' incoming messages.

Finally, one of the most significant issues this project faces is what hinders so many other ventures. *Show me the money!* Yuri Milner backed the project initially, but Breakthrough Starshot needs additional funds to get off the ground. (Pun intended!) If the money is there, the team hopes to launch in the 2030s.

NOT ONE, NOT TWO, BUT THREE STARS

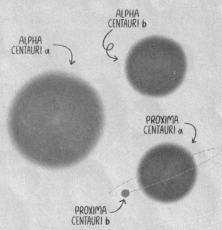

Our closest star system is the Alpha Centauri system, which consists of three stars: Alpha Centauri A, Alpha Centauri B, and Proxima Centauri. Alpha Centauri A and Alpha Centauri B orbit around their common center of gravity. (Imagine two people holding hands and spinning around an invisible center point between them.) Alpha Centauri A is slightly bigger than our Sun, and Alpha Centauri B is somewhat smaller. Because of their close proximity to each other, they appear as one star to us. It's the third-brightest spot in our night sky and is called the southern star. Proxima Centauri is a red dwarf that revolves around the other two stars and is approximately 4.2 light-years from Earth. (Proxima Centauri takes about a half million years to complete a journey around Alpha Centauri A and Alpha Centauri B.) As of now, no exoplanets have been detected around Alpha Centauri A or Alpha Centauri B. However (and luckily for Breakthrough Starshot), Proxima Centauri has one confirmed exoplanet, Proxima Centauri b, and two waiting for confirmation.

YA GOT ANY OTHER IDEAS? PROJECTS NOT IN THE WORKS

We've looked at some of the ideas scientists and engineers are currently developing, but what about the tech we see in movies? Fans of sci-fi are ready for the big ideas to become a reality. We want warp speed, wormholes, and fusion rockets. What's the progress on these?

WARP SPEED

While some use this term just to mean going really, really fast, it usually means traveling at the speed of light or faster. Ever since Chuck Yeager "broke" the sound barrier (meaning: traveling faster than sound) in 1947, some people have wondered if we could also go faster than light. Then, in the 1960s, *Star Trek* introduced "warp drive," which allowed the starship Enterprise to go multiple times faster than light speed. So when will we get this technology? *Never!* According to Einstein's theory of special relativity, it's impossible.

$$E = mc^2$$

(Perhaps the world's most famous equation and another contender for a forehead tattoo. I mean, for a T-shirt.)

E is energy, *m* is mass, and *c* is the speed of light.

In a vacuum, all light waves travel at a speed of approximately 186,000 miles (300,000 kilometers) per second. That's fast enough to circle Earth seven times in a second! Light waves do not have mass, and anything with mass (you, me, my dogs, space shuttles—even oxygen molecules) will travel slower than light, no matter how much energy we pump into the system. Warp speed looks to remain fictional.

WORMHOLES

These hypothetical bridges are space-time shortcuts. You enter at a certain location and pop out at a different location. The theory is often illustrated by imagining our universe as a piece of paper (or cloth, because sci-fi writers like to refer to "the fabric of space-time"). We are a dot on the

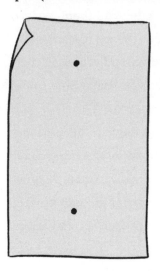

paper and want to travel to another spot, say, ten light-years away.

We already know we can't travel at the speed of light. (If we could, we'd still take ten years to get there.) But maybe there is a way to cheat and close the gap. If we could bend the space-time paper—so the dots line up closely—we would merely have to step through an opening to be in the new location. This is the idea behind wormholes.

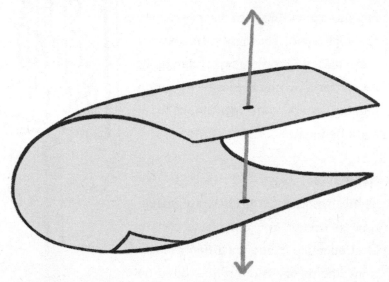

The idea was first introduced in 1916 when physicist Ludwig Flamm reviewed some solutions to Einstein's theory of general relativity equations. Flamm didn't call them wormholes; he called them white holes. About twenty years later, Einstein and Nathan Rosen looked into it and proposed that these bridges between different points in space-time *could* exist. They might be out there!

Yet none have been discovered, and they are likely to be quantumly small—like, smaller than an atom. But if a wormhole was located, perhaps it could be manipulated. Maybe the opening could be enlarged enough for human travel. Not that it would be safe! There would likely be radiation and unknown elements involved. The wormhole could also collapse or close. There's so much to worry about before we step inside one. For now, wormholes are stuck in the realm of science fiction.

FUSION ROCKETS

Essentially, these are spacecraft fueled by nuclear fusion, which is the process that fuels the Sun. We already have fusion bombs (AKA: thermonuclear bombs), but instead of obliterating the planet, perhaps fusion technology could be used to send humans into space beyond our Moon. Currently, our space programs use chemical rockets, which are heavy and relatively slow. (For example, it took Perseverance about seven months to get to Mars.) Fusion rockets would be lighter and travel at least twice as fast. Estimates say we could reach Mars in as few as 100 days, and one company's goal is for the journey to take only a month. The technology isn't quite ready yet, but several companies are looking into it, and in 2019, the US government approved $125 million to develop nuclear thermal propulsion rockets. (So technically, fusion rockets are sorta in the works, but going from concept to prototype to functioning rocket is a path riddled with near-impossible hurdles.) The hitch, of course, is that this technology is ideal only for travel *within* our solar system. Fusion rockets will not get humans to Proxima Centauri b, for example. That would still take thousands of years on a fusion rocket.

SPACE TRAVEL—WORTH THE COST?

It can be argued that traveling across our solar system and beyond is mostly about satisfying our curiosity—it's good nerdy fun, even to think about what is or isn't possible. But discovering a fossilized amoeba on Mars most likely wouldn't change our lives. We have plenty of Earthly problems that need more funding. Maybe the billions spent traveling to the Moon, Mars, and Venus could be spent on education, childhood hunger, medical science, greener forms of energy, or faster Wi-Fi. The list of needs is seemingly endless, and the impacts could be life changing for billions of people.

But an argument could also be made that we should investigate space travel because we will eventually need it. Let's assume humans survive the next billion years—though this is a big ole assumption considering no species has lasted more than a few million. If we're still around, the relatively stable environment we're used to will change rapidly. In about a billion years, the Sun will run out of its preferred core fuel, hydrogen, and will start using helium, causing our favorite star to get hotter and larger. Earth's temperature will rise and eventually surpass 700°F (370°C). All surface water will boil away. *Bye-bye, habitable planet.* Humans and their pets will need to be transported to a new home, likely outside our solar system. Depending on the size and temperature of the Sun, though, these future people and pets might be able to spend a few million years on Pluto, which could be in a new habitable zone.

While the Sun's evolution and eventual death are practically guaranteed, maybe something else will deal Earth a deadly blow within the next billion years. Killer asteroid? Out-of-control climate change? Nuclear disaster? There are many to consider. (To learn more, check out *Save the People! Halting Human Extinction* by the same author of this book you just can't put down.) We may have to abandon ship—or Earth—sooner rather than later. New technology now would only help us form an escape plan—and maybe find the aliens too.

AND WHEN IT DOES HAPPEN...

Let's imagine for a moment that some telescope somewhere finds proof of intelligent life. Maybe an easy-to-decode "hello" message or an entire *Encyclopedia Galactica*. How would astronomers go about telling the world? Turns out, the United Nations has an Office for Outer Space Affairs (UNOOSA). Its role is to make space access equitable for all Earthlings. UNOOSA also concerns itself with threats like near-Earth objects (ex: asteroids, comets, meteoroids), creates space laws (like no one is allowed to use nuclear bombs in space, and no one can own Jupiter or other space-y locations), registers launches (who is sending up rockets and when), and tackles problems like space junk (equipment, debris, or any trash humans leave in space). But if scientists discover intelligent life on a far-off planet, UNOOSA would probably hear about it the same way we would—on the internet. UNOOSA doesn't oversee anything to do with aliens (including alien communications, visitations, and invasions).

Though there are no hard-and-fast rules for reporting alien communications, the SETI community does have some guidelines, created by the SETI Permanent Study Group of the International Academy of Astronautics (IAA): *Declaration of Principles Concerning the Conduct of the Search for Extraterrestrial Intelligence.*

Rule 1: While searching for extraterrestrials, don't be super secretive. In official language, "SETI experiments will be conducted transparently."

Rule 2: When astronomers think they got something, they should ask other astronomers to check it out. *Did you hear that? It's coming from that star over there.*

Rule 3: When an astronomer is certain of a discovery, they can tell the world, specifically the public, the scientific community, and the secretary-general of the UN (who is the head of the UN and not part of the Office for Outer Space Affairs).

Rule 4: Share the necessary data with the international scientific community. Again, this is not the time to keep secrets.

Rule 5: Keep a lookout. The signal (or whatever has been discovered) needs to be watched and recorded—and then repeat rule 4.

(We'll skip rules 6 and 7 because they're too technical for our purposes.)

Rule 8: Don't reply! At least not without talking it over with others and getting permission from an international group, like the United Nations. Maybe then UNOOSA will finally take an interest in aliens. I know the rest of the world will!

We can only hope that astronomers and scientists are required to follow these procedures one day. For now, we are each still free to decide if we're team Only Earth or team Life Beyond Earth. That might not be the case in a future edition of this book.

CHAPTER 13

QUESTIONS FOR LONG CAR RIDES

I wasn't keeping track, but it feels like we've raised more questions than we've answered. Where are the aliens? Out there...maybe/probably/definitely. We just don't know *yet*. But we have hope, and it all hinges on that last word, "yet." Before we say goodbye, here are some questions (and paradoxes!) for you to ponder. You can dwell on these alone or with your friends over lunch at the Los Alamos cafeteria (or wherever you set down your food tray). There are no correct answers, making these harder than most end-of-grade test questions—but also more fun! You cannot be wrong! We might have definitive answers in the future, though. And perhaps you, inquisitive reader, could be the scientist who tells the world we're not alone.

WHAT EVIDENCE WOULD WE NEED TO CONFIRM AN ALIEN ENCOUNTER? Multiple firsthand accounts? Video? An ET being interviewed by Oprah? (For extra credit, create a list of questions for the interview.)

WHICH CAME FIRST, THE CHICKEN OR THE EGG? For bonus points, also answer, Why did the chicken cross the road?

DO YOU BELIEVE THAT ALL LIFE IS CONTAINED ON PLANET EARTH? In your answer, feel free to use math or gut feelings. Remember, there's no concrete, agreed-upon science to help you out.

IF SCIENTISTS FIND MICROSCOPIC LIFE IN OUR SOLAR SYSTEM, SHOULD THEY BRING IT BACK TO EARTH TO STUDY? Your response can be in the form of a terrifying short story.

THIS WILL BE FUN! BWAHAHAHA

HAS EARTH ALREADY BEEN VISITED BY EXTRATERRESTRIALS? Consider alien "encounters" from the past century, UAP sightings by the military, and the giant asteroid (alien bomb?) that wiped out the dinosaurs.

STACY
LIZ
SERGIÑO
NICOLE
ANTONEE
CHRISTIAN
JIYOUNG
DYLAN
OZIOMA
THE PRESIDENT

IF AND WHEN EXTRATERRESTRIAL LIFE IS CONFIRMED, WHO SHOULD BE TOLD FIRST? (I want to suggest putting my name near the top of the list.)

WOULD YOU WANT TO BE PART OF THE FIRST MARS SETTLEMENT? What if you couldn't go with your friends and family? What if it was a one-way journey?

HOW WOULD HUMANS RESPOND TO ASTROBIOLOGISTS' CLAIMS OF DISCOVERING INTELLIGENT LIFE ON AN EXOPLANET? Think of the initial reaction (which would probably include dancing in the streets, at least in front of my house), but also think of the possible responses from the government, the economy, the media, and religious institutions (recall, for example, the past issues with the heliocentric model of our solar system). Do you think you should get the day off from school (in celebration or in fear)?

TO METI OR NOT TO METI? Should we try to contact intelligent aliens? Why wait for an ET to call us when we can pick up the phone? If we did send messages into space, what should we say? What info about Earth should be included? (Our location, pictures, art, music, this book, etc.?) Create your own Golden Record.

IS THE SEARCH FOR EXTRATERRESTRIAL LIFE WORTH IT? Earth and its Earthlings have many problems and challenges. Would money and resources be better spent on other issues? Or do we need more money for space projects?

FINALLY, WHERE ARE THE ALIENS? Tell me! I want to know.

ACKNOWLEDGMENTS

Well, this was a fun, frightening, and frustrating book to write. As a kid, I wanted to be an astronaut, so taking a deep dive into space, aliens, and history was definitely fun. But some of what I learned was frightening—like both the idea that Earthlings might be alone and might not be alone. Terrifying! And I got frustrated because it seems as if NASA and other science organizations are making discoveries daily. I can't keep up, but I sure tried.

Luckily, I wasn't alone on this journey. There are many people to thank, and I must start with my editor, Liz Kossnar. She is brilliant, curious, and patient. This book would be a shell of an idea without her insight. I appreciate every email and phone call (and a lunch) where we discussed aliens. And, of course, we're supported by a fantastic team at Little, Brown: Jen Graham, Jenny Kimura, Lauren Kisare, Lisa Yoskowitz, Anna Dobbin, and the marketing, publicity, school and library, and sales departments, including Bill Grace, Andie Divelbiss, Cheryl Lew, and Christie Michel. Thank you, all!

In the fall of 2022, I put a call out on social media for beta readers, and I was overwhelmed by the volunteers. I ended up working with three educators with science backgrounds. These remarkable women read the book in a few short weeks and gave me incredible insight on making the text kid friendly and science accurate. Big thank-yous go to Cindy Perdue, Alison Hinesman from Garfield Middle School, and Jennifer Poole from Bryson Middle School.

While writing this book, I also reached out to a few scientists with questions and requests. Nearly everyone I contacted offered assistance. Thank you to Dan Werthimer of the astronomy department and Space Sciences Lab at the University of California, Berkeley, for helping me understand radio wave interference. Thank you to Tessa Fischer, astrobiologist and PhD student at the School of Earth and Space Exploration at Arizona State University, for talking me through Drake equation variables. It's hard to plug in numbers when so much is unknown. Thank you to Jen Black, chemist and one of my BFFs for fielding countless science inquiries. And infinite thanks to Jill Tarter for answering my interview questions. I never imagined I'd have the opportunity to communicate with a SETI icon. Thank you!

Of course, any mistakes found in this book are solely my fault—though unintentional.

Also, thank you to my agent, Lori Kilkelly, for handling all my publishing needs and issues—and always going above and beyond. Thank you to Bookmarks for the continued support. Thank you to Stuart Gibbs, Steve Sheinkin, and Alan Gratz for offering kind words on *Save the People!* Thank you to Nicole Miles for creating funny and informative art. And thank you to Lin-Manuel Miranda, who had nothing to do with this book (but has been mentioned in all my acknowledgments—this is the fifth time!).

While I was working on this book, Frank Drake passed away at age ninety-two. I wish I'd had the opportunity to meet him. But even so, I've enjoyed learning about the stars (and potential aliens) through his famous equation and inspiring career. RIP, Frank.

My family always contributes to my books. They don't put words to paper, and sometimes they don't even get to read the pages before they go to print. However, they are the foundation of everything I write. They listen to my ideas and suffer along with me through my writing struggles. Brett, Cora, Lily, and Henry, you mean everything to me. Mom and Glen, Dad and Suzanne, and Bob and Fran, you are the best cheerleaders a girl could have. (And an extra shout-out to the McParents for the silly dinner conversations we had while I edited this book. I promise you that aliens did not build the pyramids, regardless of what you saw on TV.) Then there are the dogs: Ray-ka, Luigi, and Munchkin. As I write this in the middle of the night, y'all are faithfully still in "our" office, lying at my feet, though it's past bedtime. Thank you, fam. I love you all!

Lastly, thank you, reader! (You may have also noticed I dedicated this book to you.) Thank you for spending time with my book—and by extension, me! I know you are very busy. Reader, maybe you are team Only Earth, or maybe you are team Life Beyond Earth. It doesn't matter to me. I just hope you are team science. Go out into the world and investigate the unknown, ask questions, and demand proof. And if you happen to discover aliens, please let me know ASAP!

TIMELINE OF EVENTS THAT ARE IMPORTANT TO THIS BOOK

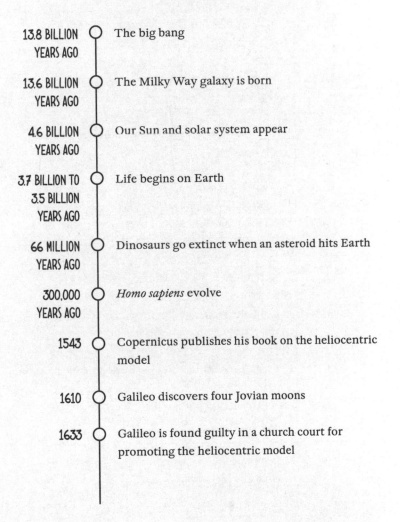

13.8 BILLION YEARS AGO	The big bang
13.6 BILLION YEARS AGO	The Milky Way galaxy is born
4.6 BILLION YEARS AGO	Our Sun and solar system appear
3.7 BILLION TO 3.5 BILLION YEARS AGO	Life begins on Earth
66 MILLION YEARS AGO	Dinosaurs go extinct when an asteroid hits Earth
300,000 YEARS AGO	*Homo sapiens* evolve
1543	Copernicus publishes his book on the heliocentric model
1610	Galileo discovers four Jovian moons
1633	Galileo is found guilty in a church court for promoting the heliocentric model

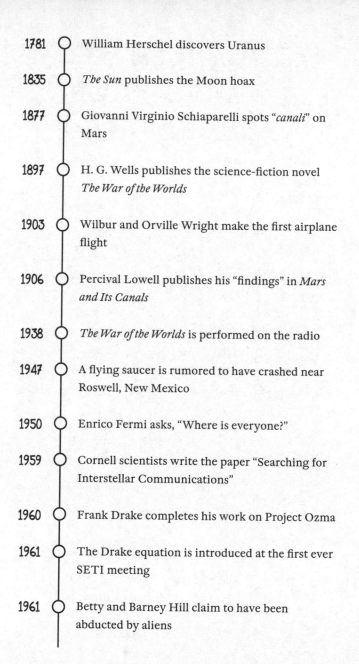

1781	○	William Herschel discovers Uranus
1835	○	*The Sun* publishes the Moon hoax
1877	○	Giovanni Virginio Schiaparelli spots *"canali"* on Mars
1897	○	H. G. Wells publishes the science-fiction novel *The War of the Worlds*
1903	○	Wilbur and Orville Wright make the first airplane flight
1906	○	Percival Lowell publishes his "findings" in *Mars and Its Canals*
1938	○	*The War of the Worlds* is performed on the radio
1947	○	A flying saucer is rumored to have crashed near Roswell, New Mexico
1950	○	Enrico Fermi asks, "Where is everyone?"
1959	○	Cornell scientists write the paper "Searching for Interstellar Communications"
1960	○	Frank Drake completes his work on Project Ozma
1961	○	The Drake equation is introduced at the first ever SETI meeting
1961	○	Betty and Barney Hill claim to have been abducted by aliens

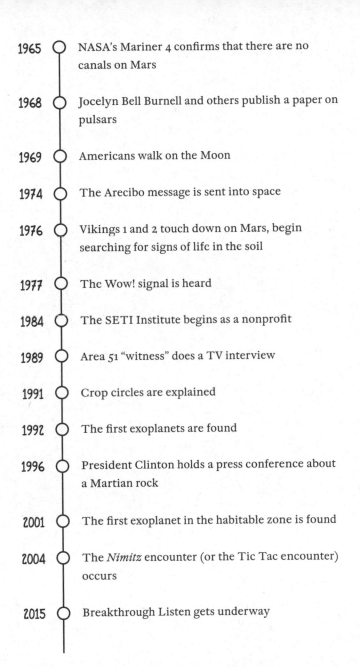

1965	NASA's Mariner 4 confirms that there are no canals on Mars
1968	Jocelyn Bell Burnell and others publish a paper on pulsars
1969	Americans walk on the Moon
1974	The Arecibo message is sent into space
1976	Vikings 1 and 2 touch down on Mars, begin searching for signs of life in the soil
1977	The Wow! signal is heard
1984	The SETI Institute begins as a nonprofit
1989	Area 51 "witness" does a TV interview
1991	Crop circles are explained
1992	The first exoplanets are found
1996	President Clinton holds a press conference about a Martian rock
2001	The first exoplanet in the habitable zone is found
2004	The *Nimitz* encounter (or the Tic Tac encounter) occurs
2015	Breakthrough Listen gets underway

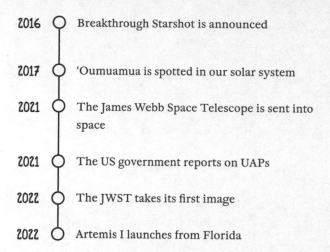

2016	Breakthrough Starshot is announced
2017	'Oumuamua is spotted in our solar system
2021	The James Webb Space Telescope is sent into space
2021	The US government reports on UAPs
2022	The JWST takes its first image
2022	Artemis I launches from Florida

ABBREVIATIONS

AATIP: Advanced Aerospace Threat Identification Program

AKA: also known as

BITG: Beacon in the Galaxy

CIA: Central Intelligence Agency

CSA: Canadian Space Agency

DNA: deoxyribonucleic acid

ECREE: "Extraordinary claims require extraordinary evidence."

ESA: European Space Agency

ET: extraterrestrial

ETI: extraterrestrial intelligence

FBI: Federal Bureau of Investigation

HabEx: Habitable Exoplanet Observatory

HRMS: High-Resolution Microwave Survey

HRP: Human Research Program

HST: Hubble Space Telescope

IAA: International Academy of Astronautics

ISS: International Space Station

JUICE: Jupiter Icy Moons Explorer

JWST: James Webb Space Telescope

LR: labeled release (experiment)

LuvEx: LUVOIR and HabEx hybrid

LUVOIR: Large Ultraviolet Optical Infrared Surveyor

METI: messaging extraterrestrial intelligence

NASA: National Aeronautics and Space Administration

NTTR: Nevada Test and Training Range

OSETI: optical search for extraterrestrial intelligence

PANOSETI: pulsed all-sky near-infrared optical SETI

RAAF: Roswell Army Air Field

RIME: Radar for Icy Moons Exploration

RNA: ribonucleic acid

ROY G. BIV: red, orange, yellow, green, blue, indigo, violet

SETI: search for extraterrestrial intelligence

TESS: Transient Exoplanet Survey Satellite

UAP: unidentified aerial phenomenon

UAPTF: Unidentified Aerial Phenomena Task Force

UFO: unidentified flying object

UNOOSA: United Nations Office for Outer Space Affairs

USG: United States government

GLOSSARY

asteroid: a space rock; can be metallic

asteroid belt: the space-rock-filled lane between Mars and Jupiter

astrobiologist: scientist who studies life and evolution around the universe

atmosphere: a blanket of gases surrounding a planet

atom: the smallest form of matter; has neutrons, protons, and electrons

autonomously: able to act independently, as in moving on its own

biologist: scientist who studies life-forms

biosignature: evidence of past or present life

canal: an artificial waterway, like the Erie, Panama, and Suez Canals

cosmic pluralism: the belief that there are worlds beyond Earth that have life

cosmonaut: a Russian (or Soviet) astronaut

dark energy: a theoretical force that opposes gravity—it may or may not exist.

erosion: the wearing away of surface material

exoplanet: a planet not in our solar system

fission: the splitting of atoms, which results in a ton of energy

fusion: the merging of atoms, creating tons and tons and tons of energy

geocentric: refers to an Earth-centered universe or solar system

geothermal activity: heat and energy coming from within a planet, dwarf planet, or moon

Goldilocks zone: fun term for "habitable zone"

gravity: an invisible force that pulls; the bigger an object, the greater the pull

habitable zone: the region around a star where liquid water can exist on the surface of an orbiting planet

heliocentric: refers to a Sun-centered universe or solar system

heresy: a belief or opinion that goes against religious opinion

Homo sapiens: our species, humans

Inquisition: in the past, the official church-run court

intelligent life: creatures who can understand and learn

intergalactic: happening between multiple galaxies

interstellar travel: journeying from one star system to another

intragalactic: happening within one galaxy

light-year: the distance light travels in a year (about 5.88 trillion miles, or 9.46 trillion kilometers)

magnetosphere: an area around a planet where magnetic fields dominate

meteorite: a rock from space that lands on our planet

microbe: a microorganism, an organism that requires a microscope to be seen

neutron star: a dead star that's 12 miles (20 kilometers) across; the densest object known in the universe

orbital time: a planet's year length; Earth's orbital time is 365 days

panspermia: a theory that suggests that life (or the building blocks of life) was brought to Earth by space rocks

pulsar: spinning neutron stars that emit precise pulses of electromagnetic waves

quasar: a bright light found in the center of some galaxies

satellite: a body orbiting a planet; can be natural or artificial

scientific consensus: when the overwhelming majority of scientists in a particular field agree with a statement

sound barrier: the obstacles associated with traveling faster than the speed of sound

snowline: the distance from a star beyond which water remains permanently frozen

technosignature: evidence of current or past technology

tidally locked: when a planet revolves and rotates at the same speed, so the same side of the planet always faces its star

vacuum: an area void of matter, even air

FAVORITE RESOURCES

WEBSITES AND VIDEOS

Kennedy's Moon Speech: https://www.jfklibrary.org/learn/about-jfk
/historic-speeches/address-at-rice-university-on-the-nations
-space-effort.

NASA's "Exoplanet Exploration." https://exoplanets.nasa.gov.

"Navy pilots describe encounters with UFOs," from *60 Minutes*. https://
youtu.be/ZBtMbBPzqHY.

Stephen Webb's "Where Are All the Aliens?" TED Talk: https://www
.ted.com/talks/stephen_webb_where_are_all_the_aliens.

For up-to-date links, visit stacymcanulty.com/alien-links.

BOOKS

Cosmos by Carl Sagan (Ballantine, 1980)

Extraterrestrial: The First Sign of Intelligent Life beyond Earth by Avi Loeb
(Houghton Mifflin Harcourt, 2021)

*In the Shadow of the Moon: America, Russia, and the Hidden History of the
Space Race* by Amy Cherrix (Balzer + Bray, 2021)

Light of the Stars: Alien Worlds and the Fate of the Earth by Adam Frank
(W. W. Norton, 2018)

Making Contact: Jill Tarter and the Search for Extraterrestrial Intelligence
by Sarah Scoles (Pegasus, 2017)

*Out There: A Scientific Guide to Alien Life, Antimatter, and Human Space
Travel (for the Cosmically Curious)* by Michael Wall, PhD (Grand
Central, 2018)

Save the People! Halting Human Extinction by Stacy McAnulty, illustrated by Nicole Miles (Little, Brown, 2022)

The Sirens of Mars: Searching for Life on Another World by Sarah Stewart Johnson (Crown, 2020)

SOURCE NOTES

CHAPTER 1

1   The universe has billions and billions of planets: National Aeronautics and Space Administration (NASA), "Beyond Our Solar System," updated July 25, 2022, https://solarsystem.nasa.gov/solar-system/beyond/overview/.

1   65 percent of American adults believe: Courtney Kennedy and Arnold Lau, "Most Americans Believe in Intelligent Life beyond Earth; Few See UFOs as a Major National Security Threat," Pew Research Center, June 30, 2021, www.pewresearch.org/fact-tank/2021/06/30/most-americans-believe-in-intelligent-life-beyond-earth-few-see-ufos-as-a-major-national-security-threat/.

2   Andromeda galaxy, 2.5 million light-years away: NASA, "The Galaxy Next Door," updated August 7, 2017, www.nasa.gov/mission_pages/galex/pia15416.html.

3   Enrico Fermi, an Italian physicist born in 1901: Lawrence Badash, "Enrico Fermi," *Encyclopedia Britannica*, updated September 25, 2022, www.britannica.com/biography/Enrico-Fermi.

4   In 1950, Fermi was working at Los Alamos: Paul Patton, "Enrico Fermi and Extraterrestrial Intelligence," Phys.org, April 8, 2015, https://phys.org/news/2015-04-enrico-fermi-extraterrestrial-intelligence.html.

7   It wasn't until the mid-1970s that this pondering: Elizabeth Howell, "Fermi Paradox: Where Are the Aliens?," Space.com, December 17, 2021, www.space.com/25325-fermi-paradox.html.

7   Sun Diameter: NASA, "Our Sun—By the Numbers," updated April 19, 2022, https://solarsystem.nasa.gov/solar-system/sun/by-the-numbers/.

7   Earth Diameter: NASA, "Our Sun—By the Numbers."

7   Jupiter Diameter: NASA, "Jupiter—By the Numbers," updated August 10, 2022, https://solarsystem.nasa.gov/planets/jupiter/by-the-numbers/.

7   To Nearest Star: Erik Gregersen, "How Do We Know How Far Away the Stars Are?," *Encyclopedia Britannica*, August 15, 2016, www.britannica.com/story/how-do-we-know-how-far-away-the-stars-are.

8   The Milky Way galaxy is about 100,000 light-years wide: Aidan Remple, "How Big Is the Milky Way?," WorldAtlas, August 1, 2022, www.worldatlas.com/space/how-big-is-the-milky-way.html.

8   The Milky Way is 13.6 billion years old: Tereza Pultarova and Daisy Dobrijevic, "Milky Way Galaxy: Everything You Need to Know about Our Cosmic Neighborhood," Space.com, September 29, 2022, www.space.com/19915-milky-way-galaxy.html.

8 Earth is about 4.54 billion years old: "Age of Earth Collection," *National Geographic*, accessed October 24, 2022, https://education.nationalgeographic.org/resource/resource-library-age-earth.

10 fastest Earthling-made spacecraft: Elizabeth Howell, "NASA's Superfast Parker Solar Probe Just Broke Its Own Speed Record at the Sun," Space.com, November 23, 2021, www.space.com/parker-solar-probe-sun-speed-record-november-2021.

11 our world now has photosynthesis: Brian Frederick Windley, "Proterozoic Eon," *Encyclopedia Britannica*, updated August 2, 2021, www.britannica.com/science/Proterozoic-Eon.

CHAPTER 1.5

15 approximately 8 billion other people: "Current World Population," Worldometer, accessed October 24, 2022, www.worldometers.info/world-population/.

15 orbits approximately 239,000 miles: National Aeronautics and Space Administration (NASA), "Earth's Moon—Overview," May 25, 2021, https://moon.nasa.gov/inside-and-out/overview/.

16 Milky Way, maybe as many as 400 billion: Pat Brennan, "Our Milky Way Galaxy: How Big Is Space?," NASA, April 2, 2019, https://exoplanets.nasa.gov/blog/1563/our-milky-way-galaxy-how-big-is-space/.

16 the universe may have as many as 200 billion galaxies: Ailsa Harvey and Elizabeth Howell, "How Many Galaxies Are There?," Space.com, February 1, 2022, www.space.com/25303-how-many-galaxies-are-in-the-universe.html.

CHAPTER 2

17 kicked off about 13.8 billion years ago: *Encyclopedia Britannica*, "Big-Bang Model," updated March 25, 2022, www.britannica.com/science/big-bang-model.

18 It doubled in size…and protons: Ailsa Harvey and Charles Q. Choi, "Our Expanding Universe: Age, History & Other Facts," Space.com, January 18, 2022, www.space.com/52-the-expanding-universe-from-the-big-bang-to-today.html.

18 but it was dark and would remain that way: Charles Q. Choi, "The Universe's Dark Ages: How Our Cosmos Survived," Space.com, October 24, 2011, www.space.com/13368-universe-dark-ages-survival-cosmos-evolution.html.

18 About 13.6 billion years ago, stars and galaxies: "Cosmic Dawn Occurred 250 to 350 Million Years after Big Bang," Phys.org, June 24, 2021, https://phys.org/news/2021-06-cosmic-dawn-million-years-big.html.

19   The expansion of the universe is often compared: National Aeronautics and Space Administration (NASA), "Universe's Expansion May Not Be the Same in All Directions," updated April 9, 2020, www.nasa.gov/mission_pages/chandra /news/universe-s-expansion-may-not-be-the-same-in-all-directions.html.

19   estimates put its diameter at 90 billion–ish light-years: Aidan Remple, "How Big Is the Universe?," WorldAtlas, June 7, 2022, www.worldatlas.com/space /how-big-is-the-universe.html.

19   Life began on Earth within the planet's: NASA, "NEO Basics," accessed October 24, 2022, https://cneos.jpl.nasa.gov/about/life_on_earth.html.

20   In the 1950s, scientists Stanley Miller and Harold Urey: Kara Rogers, "Abiogenesis," *Encyclopedia Britannica*, updated October 3, 2022, www.britannica .com/science/abiogenesis.

21   Miller and Urey used borosilicate glass flasks: Tom Hartsfield, "What the Famous Miller-Urey Experiment Got Wrong," Big Think, November 21, 2021, https://bigthink.com/hard-science/miller-urey/.

21   There's also debate about what ingredients: Douglas Fox, "Primordial Soup's On: Scientists Repeat Evolution's Most Famous Experiment," *Scientific American*, March 28, 2007, www.scientificamerican.com/article/primordial -soup-urey-miller-evolution-experiment-repeated/.

22   definition that breaks life down into a list of activities: Lynn Margulis, Carl Sagan, and Dorion Sagan, "Life—Definitions of Life—Genetic," *Encyclopedia Britannica*, updated September 5, 2022, www.britannica.com/science/life /Genetic.

22   Probably between 3.7 billion and 3.5 billion years ago: Lynn Margulis, Carl Sagan, and Dorion Sagan, "Life—Life on Earth—Evolution and the History of Life on Earth," *Encyclopedia Britannica*, updated September 5, 2022, www .britannica.com/science/life/Evolution-and-the-history-of-life-on-Earth.

22   One popular theory has life on Earth beginning: Aaron Gronstal, "Life in the Extreme: Hydrothermal Vents," NASA, November 5, 2021, https://astrobiology .nasa.gov/news/life-in-the-extreme-hydrothermal-vents/.

22   hydrothermal vents can be over 700°F: National Oceanic and Atmospheric Administration (NOAA), "What Is a Hydrothermal Vent?," updated March 10, 2022, https://oceanservice.noaa.gov/facts/vents.html.

23   life sprang forth from "warm little ponds": Lucas Brouwers, "Did Life Evolve in a 'Warm Little Pond'?," *Thoughtomics* (blog), *Scientific American*, February 16, 2012, https://blogs.scientificamerican.com/thoughtomics/did-life-evolve -in-a-warm-little-pond/.

23   While there was hardly any dry land: Aaron Gronstal, "Exposed in a Warm Little Pond," NASA, December 6, 2018, https://astrobiology.nasa.gov/news /exposed-in-a-warm-little-pond/.

24   Earth started as an "RNA world": Robert F. Service, "How Life Could Have Arisen on an 'RNA World,'" *Science*, May 11, 2022, www.science.org/content /article/how-life-could-have-arisen-rna-world.

24   Or maybe life began through panspermia: Marc Kaufman, "In Search of Panspermia," NASA, January 6, 2017, https://astrobiology.nasa.gov/news /in-search-of-panspermia/.

25   tardigrades (also known as water bears): "Creature Survives Naked in Space," Space.com, September 8, 2008, www.space.com/5817-creature-survives -naked-space.html.

CHAPTER 3

27   "planet" is derived from a Greek word: "What Makes a Planet?," *Merriam-Webster*, accessed October 24, 2022, www.merriam-webster.com/words -at-play/planet.

28   Epicurus wrote in a letter to Herodotus: Wade Roush, "The Surprisingly Long History of Speculation about Extraterrestrials," *The Wire*, July 8, 2021, https://science.thewire.in/the-sciences/for-how-long-has-humankind -contemplated-aliens/.

28   Metrodorus of Chios put it this way: Roush, "Surprisingly Long History."

29   Aristotelian physics had four elements: Anselm H. Amadio and Anthony J. P. Kenny, "Aristotle—Doctrines—Physics and Metaphysics," *Encyclopedia Britannica*, updated August 23, 2022, www.britannica.com/biography/Aristotle /Physics-and-metaphysics.

30   Polish astronomer and mathematician: Robert S. Westman, "Nicolaus Copernicus—Publication of *De Revolutionibus*," *Encyclopedia Britannica*, updated October 4, 2022, www.britannica.com/biography/Nicolaus -Copernicus/Publication-of-De-revolutionibus.

30   dedicated his book to the pope: Sheila Rabin, "Nicolaus Copernicus," *Stanford Encyclopedia of Philosophy*, updated September 13, 2019, https://plato.stanford .edu/entries/copernicus/.

31   but it would eventually be banned, in 1616: Steph Solis, "Copernicus and the Church: What the History Books Don't Say," Christian Science Monitor, February 19, 2013, www.csmonitor.com/Technology/2013/0219/Copernicus -and-the-Church-What-the-history-books-don-t-say.

31   He created a telescope that magnified: Albert Van Helden, "Galileo— Telescopic Discoveries," *Encyclopedia Britannica*, updated August 24, 2022, www.britannica.com/biography/Galileo-Galilei/Telescopic-discoveries.

31   He submitted his manuscript to the church: Albert Van Helden, "Galileo— Galileo's Copernicanism," *Encyclopedia Britannica*, updated August 24, 2022, www.britannica.com/biography/Galileo-Galilei/Galileos-Copernicanism.

32   The Catholic Church would not accept: Tony Long, "Sept. 11, 1822: Church Admits It's Not All about Us," *Wired*, September 10, 2008, www.wired .com/2008/09/sept-11-1822-church-admits-its-not-all-about-us-2/.

32 There was even a debate about life on the Sun: Matt Simon, "Fantastically Wrong: Why the Guy Who Discovered Uranus Thought There's Life on the Sun," *Wired*, August 6, 2014, www.wired.com/2014/08/fantastically-wrong -life-on-the-sun/.

32 William Herschel, the astronomer who discovered Uranus: *Encyclopedia Britannica*, "William Herschel," updated August 21, 2022, www.britannica.com /biography/William-Herschel.

33 his son John benefited from a world-class education: *Encyclopedia Britannica*, "Sir John Herschel, 1st Baronet," updated May 7, 2022, www.britannica.com /biography/John-Herschel.

33 By August 1835, John Herschel had been busy: *Encyclopedia Britannica*, "Sir John Herschel."

34 a newspaper called *The Sun*...exotic creatures: Meg Matthias, "The Great Moon Hoax of 1835 Was Sci-Fi Passed Off as News," *Encyclopedia Britannica*, July 22, 2021, www.britannica.com/story/the-great-moon-hoax-of-1835-was -sci-fi-passed-off-as-news.

34 "Vespertilio-homo" (or man bats): Sarah Zielinski, "The Great Moon Hoax Was Simply a Sign of Its Time," *Smithsonian*, July 2, 2015, www.smithsonian mag.com/smithsonian-institution/great-moon-hoax-was-simply-sign-its -time-180955761/.

34 "probable and possible": Matthias, "Great Moon Hoax of 1835."

CHAPTER 4

36 On December 14, 1903, Wilbur and Orville Wright: Tom D. Crouch, "Wright Brothers—Powered, Sustained Flight," *Encyclopedia Britannica*, updated February 11, 2021, www.britannica.com/biography/Wright-brothers /Powered-sustained-flight.

37 the Boeing 787 Dreamliner: "Boeing 787 Dreamliner," accessed October 24, 2022, www.boeing.com/commercial/787/.

37 On October 4, 1957, the Moon: *Encyclopedia Britannica*, "Sputnik," updated March 14, 2022, www.britannica.com/technology/Sputnik.

37 the Moon is over 230,000 miles: National Aeronautics and Space Administration (NASA), "Earth's Moon—Overview," May 25, 2021, https://moon.nasa .gov/inside-and-out/overview/.

38 Sputnik 2 launched on November 3, 1957: Robert Lewis, "Laika," *Encyclopedia Britannica*, updated October 30, 2022, www.britannica.com/topic/Laika.

38 At first, they called her Kudryavka: Alex Wellerstein, "Remembering Laika, Space Dog and Soviet Hero," *New Yorker*, November 3, 2017, www.newyorker .com/tech/annals-of-technology/remembering-laika-space-dog-and-soviet -hero.

38   Sputnik 2 weighed…monitoring the dog: NASA, "Sputnik 2," October 28, 2022, https://nssdc.gsfc.nasa.gov/nmc/spacecraft/display.action?id=1957-002A.

39   only five or six hours: Lewis, "Laika."

39   In June 1948, a rhesus monkey named Albert: Mike Wall, "Monkeys in Space: A Brief Spaceflight History," Space.com, January 28, 2013, www.space.com/19505-space-monkeys-chimps-history.html.

39   The space line is arbitrary but often considered: National Environmental Satellite Data and Information Service, "Where Is Space?," February 22, 2016, www.nesdis.noaa.gov/news/where-space.

40   On December 6, 1957, the US attempted: NASA, "60 Years Ago: Vanguard Fails to Reach Orbit," updated January 30, 2018, www.nasa.gov/feature/60-years-ago-vanguard-fails-to-reach-orbit.

40   On January 31, 1958, the US successfully: NASA, "Explorer 1 Overview," updated August 3, 2017, www.nasa.gov/mission_pages/explorer/explorer-overview.html.

40   mere eighty-four days: Jake Parks, "Explorer 1: The Start of the American Space Age," *Astronomy*, January 31, 2018, https://astronomy.com/news/2018/01/explorer-1.

40   Explorer 1 orbited Earth: NASA, "Explorer 1 Overview."

40   It was the first satellite to make a scientific discovery: *Encyclopedia Britannica*, "Explorer," updated March 19, 2019, www.britannica.com/technology/Explorer-satellites.

41   Explorer 2…Explorer 5: NASA, "NASA's Explorer Program Satellites," updated December 16, 2021, https://nssdc.gsfc.nasa.gov/multi/explorer.html.

41   The Sputnik 5 capsule carried two dogs: Tony Reichhardt, "Remembering Belka and Strelka," *Smithsonian*, August 19, 2010, www.smithsonianmag.com/air-space-magazine/remembering-belka-and-strelka-143143843/.

41   on the fourth lap, Belka vomited: Richard Hollingham, "The Stray Dogs That Led the Space Race," BBC Future, November 1, 2017, www.bbc.com/future/article/20171027-the-stray-dogs-that-paved-the-way-to-the-stars.

42   Yuri Gagarin—April 12, 1961: National Archives and Records Administration, "Space Exploration," last reviewed August 21, 2016, www.archives.gov/research/alic/reference/space-timeline.html.

42   Valentina Tereshkova—June 16, 1963: *Encyclopedia Britannica*, "Valentina Tereshkova," updated November 7, 2022, www.britannica.com/biography/Valentina-Tereshkova.

43   "We choose to go to the Moon": John F. Kennedy, "Address at Rice University on the Nation's Space Effort" (Rice University, Houston, TX, September 12, 1962), transcript, JFK Library, accessed October 24, 2022, www.jfklibrary.org/learn/about-jfk/historic-speeches/address-at-rice-university-on-the-nations-space-effort.

43   Soviet Alexei Leonov took the first spacewalk: "The First Space Walk," *New Scientist,* accessed October 24, 2022, www.newscientist.com/definition/first -space-walk/.

43   American astronaut Ed White: Space Center Houston, "This Day in History: Ed White Becomes First American to Walk in Space," June 3, 2021, https:// spacecenter.org/this-day-in-history-ed-white-becomes-first-american-to -walk-in-space/.

44   Luna 9 touched down on February 3, 1966: NASA, "Luna 9," October 28, 2022, https://nssdc.gsfc.nasa.gov/nmc/spacecraft/display.action?id=1966 -006A.

44   Surveyor 1 sent back more than 11,000 pictures: NASA, "Surveyor 1," updated August 11, 2019, https://solarsystem.nasa.gov/missions/surveyor-1.

44   the Human Research Program (HRP): NASA, "About HRP," updated June 10, 2021, www.nasa.gov/hrp/about.

44   In March 2015, the agency had a unique opportunity: Ashley Strickland, "Human Health Can Be 'Mostly Sustained' for a Year in Space, NASA Twins Study Concludes," CNN, April 11, 2019, www.cnn.com/2019/04/11/health /nasa-kelly-twins-study-results.

46   the USA won on July 20, 1969: NASA, "July 20, 1969: One Giant Leap for Mankind," updated July 20, 2021, www.nasa.gov/mission_pages/apollo /apollo11.html.

46   Mariner 4 (USA): Tim Wallace, "First Mission to Mars: Mariner 4's Special Place in History," *Cosmos,* July 14, 2017, https://cosmosmagazine.com/space /first-mission-to-mars-mariner-4s-special-place-in-history/.

46   Salyut 1 (USSR): Nola Taylor Tillman, "Salyut 1: The First Space Station," Space.com, July 26, 2012, www.space.com/16773-first-space-station-salyut-1 .html.

46   Mars 3 (USSR): NASA, "A Chronology of Mars Exploration," updated April 16, 2015, www.history.nasa.gov/marschro.htm.

46   Pioneer 10 (USA): NASA, "Pioneer 10," updated July 19, 2021, https://solarsystem .nasa.gov/missions/pioneer-10.

46   Skylab (USA): David M. Harland, "Skylab," *Encyclopedia Britannica,* updated September 14, 2022, www.britannica.com/topic/Skylab.

47   Venera 9 (USSR): NASA, "Venera 9 Descent Craft," October 28, 2022, https:// nssdc.gsfc.nasa.gov/nmc/spacecraft/display.action?id=1975-050D.

47   The Venera 9 lander operated for only: NASA, "Venera 9," updated June 18, 2019, https://solarsystem.nasa.gov/missions/venera-9.

47   Viking 1 and Viking 2 (USA): NASA, "Viking 1 & 2," September 7, 2019, https://mars.nasa.gov/mars-exploration/missions/viking-1-2/.

47   Voyager 2 and Voyager 1 (USA): NASA, "Voyager—Fast Facts," accessed October 24, 2022, https://voyager.jpl.nasa.gov/frequently-asked-questions /fast-facts/.

48   Columbia (USA): Daisy Dobrijevic and Elizabeth Howell, "Space Shuttle
          Columbia: NASA's First Shuttle in Space," Space.com, October 26, 2021, www
          .space.com/18008-space-shuttle-columbia.html.

48   Hubble Space Telescope (USA and ESA, European Space Agency): Hubble
          Site, "About the Telescope," accessed December 1, 2022, https://hubblesite
          .org/about.

49   International Space Station, or ISS: ISS National Laboratory, "History and
          Timeline of the ISS," accessed October 24, 2022, www.issnationallab.org
          /about/iss-timeline/.

49   US-only project named Freedom: David M. Harland, "International Space
          Station," *Encyclopedia Britannica*, updated October 18, 2022, www.britannica
          .com/topic/International-Space-Station.

CHAPTER 5

50   African Elephants = 415,000-ish: World Wildlife Fund, "African Elephant,"
          accessed October 24, 2022, www.worldwildlife.org/species/african-elephant.

50   Chimpanzees (our closest relatives) = fewer than 250,000: World Wildlife
          Fund, "Chimpanzees," accessed October 24, 2022, https://wwf.panda.org
          /discover/knowledge_hub/endangered_species/great_apes/chimpanzees/.

51   Polar Bears = nearly 26,000: Polar Bears International, "Status," accessed
          October 24, 2022, https://polarbearsinternational.org/polar-bears-changing
          -arctic/polar-bear-facts/status/.

51   Black Rhinos = around 5,500: World Wildlife Fund, "Black Rhino," accessed
          October 24, 2022, www.worldwildlife.org/species/black-rhino.

51   Tigers = about 4,500: World Wildlife Fund, "Tiger," accessed October 24,
          2022, www.worldwildlife.org/species/tiger.

51   Giant Pandas = under 2,000: World Wildlife Fund, "Giant Panda," accessed
          October 24, 2022, www.worldwildlife.org/species/giant-panda.

51   There are about 33 billion of them: M. Shahbandeh, "Number of Chickens
          Worldwide from 1990 to 2020," Statista, January 21, 2022, www.statista.com
          /statistics/263962/number-of-chickens-worldwide-since-1990/.

51   One teaspoon of productive soil: James J. Hoorman, "Role of Soil Bacteria,"
          Ohio State University Extension, June 6, 2016, https://ohioline.osu.edu
          /factsheet/anr-36.

51   In my gut alone: Harvard Health, "Can Gut Bacteria Improve Your Health?,"
          October 14, 2016, www.health.harvard.edu/staying-healthy/can-gut-bacteria
          -improve-your-health.

52   astrobiologists are on the hunt: Robert Tindol, "Astrobiologists Should Look
          for Both Water and Energy Sources When Searching for Life on Other Worlds,
          Researcher Says," Caltech, Division of Biology and Biological Engineering,
          February 19, 2000, www.bbe.caltech.edu/news/astrobiologists-should-look
          -both-water-and-energy-sources-when-searching-life-other-worlds-382.

52   scientists have ruled out the giants: Elizabeth Howell, "Gas Giants: Jovian Planets of Our Solar System and Beyond," Space.com, March 10, 2022, www.space.com/30372-gas-giants.html.

52   Mercury is too close to the Sun: National Aeronautics and Space Administration (NASA), "Mercury," updated September 23, 2021, https://solarsystem.nasa.gov/planets/mercury/overview/.

52   This planet is known as Earth's twin: NASA, "Venus—In Depth," updated August 3, 2021, https://solarsystem.nasa.gov/planets/venus/in-depth/.

52   Venus is hot enough to melt lead: National Oceanic and Atmospheric Administration (NOAA), "The Planet Venus," March 13, 2015, www.weather.gov/fsd/venus.

53   there's just not enough water vapor: Tereza Pultarova, "Life on Venus Is Impossible Because of Lack of Water, Study Suggests," *Scientific American*, June 30, 2021, www.scientificamerican.com/article/life-on-venus-is-impossible-because-of-lack-of-water-study-suggests/.

53   This dwarf planet—please don't come at me: NASA, "Pluto—In Depth," updated August 6, 2021, https://solarsystem.nasa.gov/planets/dwarf-planets/pluto/in-depth/.

53   This dwarf planet is located in the asteroid belt: NASA, "Ceres—In Depth," updated August 5, 2021, https://solarsystem.nasa.gov/planets/dwarf-planets/ceres/in-depth/.

53   about a quarter of the size of our Moon: Edward F. Tedesco, "Ceres," *Encyclopedia Britannica*, updated January 27, 2022, www.britannica.com/place/Ceres-dwarf-planet.

54   in 2017, the NASA spacecraft Dawn: NASA, "Dawn Discovers Evidence for Organic Material on Ceres," updated August 6, 2017, www.nasa.gov/feature/jpl/dawn-discovers-evidence-for-organic-material-on-ceres.

54   Jupiter has a swarm of eighty moons: NASA, "Jupiter Moons—In Depth," updated September 23, 2022, https://solarsystem.nasa.gov/moons/jupiter-moons/in-depth/.

55   Smaller than our Moon, Europa is covered: NASA, "Thick or Thin Ice Shell on Europa?," updated May 11, 2022, https://europa.nasa.gov/resources/36/thick-or-thin-ice-shell-on-europa/.

55   According to NASA, Europa might: NASA, "Europa—Overview," updated November 4, 2021, https://solarsystem.nasa.gov/moons/jupiter-moons/europa/overview/.

55   The moon's surface also rises and falls: NASA, "Io—In Depth," updated July 19, 2021, https://solarsystem.nasa.gov/moons/jupiter-moons/io/in-depth/.

55   400 active volcanoes: Paul Scott Anderson, "Wow! New Volcano on Jupiter's Moon Io," *EarthSky*, July 23, 2018, https://earthsky.org/space/new-hot-spot-on-io-active-volcano/.

55   This giant moon is the largest: NASA, "Ganymede—In Depth," updated November 10, 2021, https://solarsystem.nasa.gov/moons/jupiter-moons/ganymede/in-depth/.

55   Jupiter's second-largest moon: NASA, "Callisto—In Depth," updated July 19, 2021, https://solarsystem.nasa.gov/moons/jupiter-moons/callisto/in-depth/.

56   tidal heating (also called tidal flexing): NASA, "An Orbital Dance May Help Preserve Oceans on Icy Worlds," updated November 30, 2017, www.nasa.gov /press-release/goddard/2017/dance-preserves-oceans.

57   Saturn's largest moon: NASA, "Titan—In Depth," updated February 4, 2021, https://solarsystem.nasa.gov/moons/saturn-moons/titan/in-depth/.

57   The moon's surface pressure: William B. Hubbard and Bonnie Buratti, "Titan— The Atmosphere," *Encyclopedia Britannica*, updated December 13, 2021, www. britannica.com/place/Titan-astronomy/The-atmosphere.

57   Another of Saturn's moons: NASA, "Enceladus," updated December 19, 2019, https://solarsystem.nasa.gov/moons/saturn-moons/enceladus/.

58   This frozen moon of Neptune: Nola Taylor Redd, "What Lies beneath Triton's Ice," *Astronomy*, August 6, 2019, https://astronomy.com/magazine /2019/08/what-lies-beneath-tritons-ice.

CHAPTER 6

59   Martian enthusiasm got a boost in 1877: *Encyclopedia Britannica*, "Canals of Mars," updated December 18, 2006, www.britannica.com/place/canals-of -Mars.

59   Schiaparelli also noted dark spots: National Aeronautics and Space Administration (NASA), "The 'Canali' and the First Martians," updated April 13, 2009, www.nasa.gov/audience/forstudents/postsecondary/features/F_Canali_and _First_Martians.html.

60   the 100-plus straight lines: *Encyclopedia Britannica*, "Canals of Mars."

60   Also, a trick of the human brain: NASA, "'Canali' and the First Martians."

60   Percival Lowell was born to a wealthy family: *Encyclopedia Britannica*, "Percival Lowell," updated November 8, 2022, www.britannica.com/biography /Percival-Lowell.

60   "as far actually as from Boston to San Francisco": Percival Lowell, *Mars and Its Canals* (Macmillan, 1906), www.gutenberg.org/files/47015/47015 -h/47015-h.htm.

61   H. G. Wells wrote the science-fiction story: Haley Bracken, "The War of the Worlds," *Encyclopedia Britannica*, updated September 1, 2022, www .britannica.com/topic/The-War-of-the-Worlds-novel-by-Wells.

61   And the classic green-skinned Martian: NASA, "'Canali' and the First Martians."

61   One of the most infamous Mars stories: A. Brad Schwartz, "The Infamous 'War of the Worlds' Radio Broadcast Was a Magnificent Fluke," *Smithsonian*, May 6, 2015, www.smithsonianmag.com/history/infamous-war-worlds -radio-broadcast-was-magnificent-fluke-180955180/.

62   He died in 1916: *Encyclopedia Britannica*, "Percival Lowell."

62   a heat ray, and poisonous black smoke: "'The War of the Worlds' Radio Script
        from October 30, 1938," Wellesnet, October 9, 2013, www.wellesnet.com/the
        -war-of-the-worlds-radio-script/.

63   Orson Welles found himself in the middle: Schwartz, "Infamous 'War of the
        Worlds' Radio Broadcast."

63   Some estimates say that 12 million Americans: Mark Memmott, "75 Years
        Ago, 'War of the Worlds' Started a Panic. Or Did It?," NPR, October 30, 2013,
        www.npr.org/sections/thetwo-way/2013/10/30/241797346/75-years-ago-war
        -of-the-worlds-started-a-panic-or-did-it.

63   less than 2 percent of those with radios: Jefferson Pooley and Michael J.
        Socolow, "The Myth of the *War of the Worlds* Panic," *Slate*, October 28, 2013,
        https://slate.com/culture/2013/10/orson-welles-war-of-the-worlds-panic
        -myth-the-infamous-radio-broadcast-did-not-cause-a-nationwide-hysteria
        .html.

64   The canal debate (and the resulting intelligent-life-on-Mars debate): Mark
        Strauss, "Why NASA's First Good Look at Mars Almost Ended Its Explora-
        tion," *National Geographic*, November 28, 2016, www.nationalgeographic
        .com/science/article/mars-exploration-nasa-mariner.

64   labeled release (LR) experiment: Ker Than, "Life on Mars Found by NASA's
        Viking Mission?," *National Geographic*, April 15, 2012, www.nationalgeographic
        .com/science/article/120413-nasa-viking-program-mars-life-space-science.

65   Some astrobiologists believe that a chemical reaction: Clara Moskowitz,
        "Looking for Life on Mars: Viking Experiment Team Member Reflects on
        Divisive Findings," *Scientific American*, April 2, 2019, www.scientificamerican
        .com/article/looking-for-life-on-mars-viking-experiment-team-member
        -reflects-on-divisive-findings/.

65   The official NASA stance is nope: NASA, "NASA's Viking Data Lives On,
        Inspires 40 Years Later," updated August 6, 2017, www.nasa.gov/feature
        /goddard/2016/nasas-viking-data-lives-on-inspires-40-years-later.

66   The story begins on Antarctica: Jo Marchant, "Life on Mars: The Story of
        Meteorite ALH84001," *BBC Science Focus*, September 15, 2020, www.science
        focus.com/space/life-on-mars-the-story-of-meteorite-alh84001/.

67   "Today, rock 84001 speaks to us": Bill Clinton, "President Clinton Statement
        regarding Mars Meteorite Discovery" (Washington, DC, August 7, 1996),
        transcript, NASA, accessed October 24, 2022, www2.jpl.nasa.gov/snc/clinton
        .html.

67   And research published in 2022 confirms: Daniella Scalice, "An Update from
        ALH84001," NASA, updated November 10, 2022, https://astrobiology.nasa
        .gov/news/an-update-from-alh84001/.

67   Landed July 4, 1997: NASA, "Mars Pathfinder," September 7, 2019, https://
        mars.nasa.gov/mars-exploration/missions/pathfinder/.

67   Dead on arrival December 3, 1999: NASA, "Mars Polar Lander/Deep Space

2," August 19, 2020, https://mars.nasa.gov/mars-exploration/missions/polar-lander/.

68   the lander crashed due to a problem: NASA, "Mars Polar Lander/Deep Space 2," updated July 25, 2019, https://solarsystem.nasa.gov/missions/mars-polar-lander-deep-space-2/in-depth/.

68   Spirit landed on January 4, 2004: NASA, "Mars Exploration Rovers," September 7, 2019, https://mars.nasa.gov/mars-exploration/missions/mars-exploration-rovers/.

68   Opportunity sent its last transmission: NASA, "Opportunity's Last Message," accessed October 24, 2022, https://mars.nasa.gov/resources/22339/opportunitys-last-message/.

69   Arrived May 25, 2008: NASA, "Mars Phoenix," September 7, 2019, https://mars.nasa.gov/mars-exploration/missions/phoenix/.

69   Phoenix used a probe: NASA, "NASA Spacecraft Confirms Martian Water, Mission Extended," updated July 31, 2008, www.nasa.gov/mission_pages/phoenix/news/phoenix-20080731.html.

69   Landed August 6, 2012: NASA, "Mars Science Laboratory," September 7, 2019, https://mars.nasa.gov/mars-exploration/missions/mars-science-laboratory/.

69   "found chemical and mineral evidence": NASA, "Mars Science Laboratory: Curiosity," accessed October 24, 2022, https://mars.nasa.gov/mars-exploration/overlay-curiosity/.

69   Touched down on February 18, 2021: NASA, "Mars 2020 Perseverance Rover," updated February 2021, https://mars.nasa.gov/mars-exploration/missions/mars2020/.

70   NASA's current plan starts with Artemis: NASA, "Artemis," accessed October 24, 2022, www.nasa.gov/specials/artemis/.

70   Artemis II will take astronauts: NASA, "First Flight with Crew Important Step on Long-Term Return to the Moon, Missions to Mars," updated October 8, 2021, www.nasa.gov/feature/nasa-s-first-flight-with-crew-important-step-on-long-term-return-to-the-moon-missions-to.

70   Artemis III will involve a Moon landing: Eleanor Lutz, "How 3 NASA Missions Could Send Astronauts Back to the Moon," *New York Times*, updated September 3, 2022, www.nytimes.com/interactive/2022/08/27/science/nasa-moon-artemis-launch.html.

70   late 2030s or early 2040s: Elizabeth Howell, "NASA Shows Off Early Plans to Send Astronauts to Mars for 30 Days," Space.com, May 24, 2022, www.space.com/nasa-plans-astronauts-mars-mission-30-days.

71   China also recently announced: Ryan Woo and Liangping Gao, "China Plans Its First Crewed Mission to Mars in 2033," Reuters, June 24, 2021, www.reuters.com/business/aerospace-defense/china-plans-its-first-crewed-mission-mars-2033-2021-06-24/.

CHAPTER 7

72   G-type yellow dwarf star: Kenneth Lang and Harold Zirin, "Sun," *Encyclopedia Britannica*, updated November 9, 2022, www.britannica.com/place/Sun.

74   But it wasn't until 1992: National Aeronautics and Space Administration (NASA), "Historic Timeline—First Exoplanets Discovered," accessed December 1, 2022, https://exoplanets.nasa.gov/alien-worlds/historic-timeline/#first-exoplanets-discovered.

74   over 5,000 exoplanets have been confirmed: NASA, "Exoplanet Exploration: Planets beyond Our Solar System," accessed December 1, 2022, https://exoplanets.nasa.gov/.

74   Transit Method...Direct Imaging: NASA, "5 Ways to Find a Planet," accessed December 1, 2022, https://exoplanets.nasa.gov/alien-worlds/ways-to-find-a-planet.

78   These are the smallest exoplanets: NASA, "Terrestrial," updated April 13, 2022, https://exoplanets.nasa.gov/what-is-an-exoplanet/planet-types/terrestrial/.

78   These exoplanets are two to ten times bigger: NASA, "Super-Earth," updated April 13, 2022, https://exoplanets.nasa.gov/what-is-an-exoplanet/planet-types/super-earth/.

78   Exoplanets in this category are like Neptune: NASA, "Neptune-Like," updated April 13, 2022, https://exoplanets.nasa.gov/what-is-an-exoplanet/planet-types/neptune-like/.

79   Naming planets usually begins: NASA, "How Do Exoplanets Get Their Names?," accessed October 24, 2022, https://exoplanets.nasa.gov/faq/20/how-do-exoplanets-get-their-names/.

79   The last category is for the big guys: NASA, "Gas Giant," updated April 13, 2022, https://exoplanets.nasa.gov/what-is-an-exoplanet/planet-types/gas-giant/.

80   This is the region around a star: NASA, "The Search for Life—The Habitable Zone," updated April 2, 2021, https://exoplanets.nasa.gov/search-for-life/habitable-zone/.

81   Venus is at the inner ring: NASA, "What Is the Habitable Zone?," updated March 10, 2021, https://exoplanets.nasa.gov/resources/2255/what-is-the-habitable-zone/.

81   Only the right kind of star: Paul Scott Anderson, "Goldilocks Stars Best for Alien Life?," *EarthSky*, January 23, 2020, https://earthsky.org/space/goldilocks-stars-g-k-dwarfs-best-for-alien-life/.

81   which is 71 percent water: Water Science School, "How Much Water Is There on Earth?," US Geological Survey, November 13, 2019, www.usgs.gov/special-topics/water-science-school/science/how-much-water-there-earth.

82   home to 15 percent of all Earthly life: Hannah Ritchie, "Oceans, Land and Deep Subsurface: How Is Life Distributed across Environments?," Our World in Data, April 26, 2019, https://ourworldindata.org/life-by-environment.

82   water vapor has been detected: NASA, "A Hubble First: Water Vapor Found on Habitable-Zone Exoplanet," updated September 21, 2020, https://exoplanets.nasa.gov/news/1600/a-hubble-first-water-vapor-found-on-habitable-zone-exoplanet/.

82   more than 25 percent of exoplanets: Lonnie Shekhtman, "Are Planets with Oceans Common in the Galaxy? It's Likely, NASA Scientists Find," NASA, June 18, 2020, www.nasa.gov/feature/goddard/2020/are-planets-with-oceans-common-in-the-galaxy-it-s-likely-nasa-scientists-find.

82   nitrogen (78 percent) and oxygen (21 percent): Jonathan I. Lunine, Raymond Jeanloz, and Clark R. Chapman, "Earth—The Atmosphere and Hydrosphere," *Encyclopedia Britannica*, updated October 18, 2022, www.britannica.com/place/Earth/The-atmosphere.

82   burn up in the mesosphere: Alan Buis, "Earth's Atmosphere: A Multi-layered Cake," NASA, October 2, 2019, https://climate.nasa.gov/news/2919/earths-atmosphere-a-multi-layered-cake/.

82   The composition of an exoplanet's atmosphere: NASA, "What's a Transit?," accessed October 24, 2022, https://exoplanets.nasa.gov/faq/31/whats-a-transit/.

83   Plate tectonics are vital: Shannon Hall, "Earth's Tectonic Activity May Be Crucial for Life—and Rare in Our Galaxy," *Scientific American*, July 20, 2017, www.scientificamerican.com/article/earths-tectonic-activity-may-be-crucial-for-life-and-rare-in-our-galaxy/.

83   strong evidence of plate tectonics on LHS 3844 b: Kelly Kizer Whitt, "First Exoplanet with Evidence of Tectonics," *EarthSky*, March 11, 2021, https://earthsky.org/space/exoplanet-lhs-3844b-hemisphere-volcano-tectonics/.

84   Terrestrial and smaller super-Earth exoplanets: Paul Sutter, "Just How Big Can a Super-Earth Get While Staying 'Habitable'?," Space.com, August 4, 2022, www.space.com/super-earth-exoplanet-habitability-size-constraints.

84   It prevents Earth from wobbling on its axis: NASA, "Earth's Moon," updated July 27, 2022, https://solarsystem.nasa.gov/moons/earths-moon/overview/.

84   a few possible exomoons being investigated: Jonathan O'Callaghan, "Astronomers Have Found Another Possible 'Exomoon' beyond Our Solar System," *Scientific American*, January 13, 2022, www.scientificamerican.com/article/astronomers-have-found-another-possible-exomoon-beyond-our-solar-system/.

85   a protective magnetosphere: Alan Buis, "Earth's Magnetosphere: Protecting Our Planet from Harmful Space Energy," NASA, August 3, 2021, https://climate.nasa.gov/news/3105/earths-magnetosphere-protecting-our-planet-from-harmful-space-energy/.

85   whether an exoplanet has a solid core: Matt Williams, "One of the TRAPPIST-1 Planets Has an Iron Core," Universe Today, May 3, 2018, www.universetoday.com/139155/one-of-the-trappist-1-planets-has-an-iron-core/.

85   Exoplanet temperatures cannot be directly measured: NASA, "What Is an Exoplanet?," updated April 2, 2021, https://exoplanets.nasa.gov/what-is-an -exoplanet/overview/.

86   Temperature and Color: NASA, "What Is an Exoplanet?—Stars," updated April 13, 2022, https://exoplanets.nasa.gov/what-is-an-exoplanet/stars/.

86   Size and Brightness: "The Classification of Stars," Atlas of the Universe, accessed October 24, 2022, http://www.atlasoftheuniverse.com/startype.html.

86   Up to 1,000,000 times greater than our Sun: Encyclopedia Britannica, "Supergiant Star," updated April 13, 2016, www.britannica.com/science/supergiant -star.

86   Main sequence stars can be smaller: Nola Taylor Tillman and Ben Biggs, "Main Sequence Stars: Definition & Life Cycle," Space.com, January 26, 2022, www.space.com/22437-main-sequence-star.html.

87   In 2001, the first exoplanet: NASA, "Historic Timeline—First Planet Found within the 'Habitable Zone,'" accessed December 1, 2022, https://exoplanets. nasa.gov/alien-worlds/historic-timeline/#first-planet-found-within-the -habitable-zone.

87   128 light-years from Earth: NASA, "Exoplanet Catalog—HD 28185 b," accessed October 24, 2022, https://exoplanets.nasa.gov/exoplanet-catalog /6606/hd-28185-b/.

87   It is considered uninhabitable: European Southern Observatory, "Exoplanets: The Hunt Continues!," April 4, 2001, www.eso.org/public/usa/news /eso0114/.

87   This super-Earth exoplanet is speedy: NASA, "Exoplanet Catalog— Teegarden's Star b," accessed October 24, 2022, https://exoplanets.nasa.gov /exoplanet-catalog/7423/teegardens-star-b/.

87   the habitable zone of a gentle red dwarf: Nadia Drake, "Two Potentially 87Life-Friendly Planets Found Orbiting a Nearby Star," National Geographic, June 18, 2019, www.nationalgeographic.com/science/article/two-potentially -life-friendly-planets-found-12-light-years-away-teegardens-star.

88   It's twelve light-years from us: NASA, "Exoplanet Catalog—Teegarden's Star b."

88   This exoplanet is also a super-Earth: Jeanette Kazmierczak, "NASA Planet Hunter Finds Its 1st Earth-Size Habitable-Zone World," NASA, updated December 18, 2020, www.nasa.gov/feature/goddard/2020/nasa-planet-hunter -finds-its-1st-earth-size-habitable-zone-world.

89   This is our nearest exoplanet: NASA, "Proxima b 3D Model," updated September 21, 2020, https://exoplanets.nasa.gov/resources/2211/proxima -b-3d-model/.

89   "NASA's Kepler mission has confirmed": NASA, "NASA's Kepler Mission Discovers Bigger, Older Cousin to Earth," updated August 7, 2017, www.nasa .gov/press-release/nasa-kepler-mission-discovers-bigger-older-cousin -to-earth.

89   about 6 billion years old: Erik Gregersen, "Kepler-452b," *Encyclopedia Britannica*, updated June 19, 2018, www.britannica.com/place/Kepler-452b.

89   the magnificent seven of TRAPPIST-1: NASA, "Largest Batch of Earth-Size Habitable Zone Planets Found Orbiting TRAPPIST-1," updated February 15, 2022, https://exoplanets.nasa.gov/trappist1/.

90   Here's what they came up with: Dirk Schulze-Makuch, René Heller, and Edward Guinan, "In Search for a Planet Better Than Earth: Top Contenders for a Superhabitable World," *Astrobiology* 20, no. 12 (December 2020), https://doi.org/10.1089/ast.2019.2161; and Charles Q. Choi, "Superhabitable Planets: Alien Worlds That May Be More Habitable Than Earth," Space.com, February 24, 2022, www.space.com/superhabitable-planets.

90   Of the thousands of known exoplanets: Choi, "Superhabitable Planets."

CHAPTER 8

93   The year was 1961: John Wenz, "The Secret Origins of the Search for Extraterrestrial Intelligence," *Discover*, February 11, 2019, www.discovermagazine.com/the-sciences/the-secret-origins-of-the-search-for-extraterrestrial-intelligence.

93   Drake realized he needed some structure: Nadia Drake, "Why Alien Hunters Have Spent 60 Years Finding New Solutions for the Drake Equation," *National Geographic*, November 30, 2021, www.nationalgeographic.com/science/article/why-alien-hunters-have-spent-60-years-finding-new-solutions-for-the-drake-equation.

94   Meet the Drake Equation: *Encyclopedia Britannica*, "Drake Equation," updated June 3, 2022, www.britannica.com/science/Drake-equation.

94   the estimated rate varies from one to seven: Kerry Hensley, "Solving a Fifty-Year Star-Formation Mystery," AAS Nova, April 25, 2022, https://aasnova.org/2022/04/25/solving-a-fifty-year-star-formation-mystery/; and Christopher Wanjek, "Milky Way Churns Out Seven New Stars per Year, Scientists Say," National Aeronautics and Space Administration (NASA), updated February 23, 2008, www.nasa.gov/centers/goddard/news/topstory/2006/milkyway_seven.html.

95   Now astronomers know they're the norm: Mike Wall, "Nearly Every Star Hosts at Least One Alien Planet," Space.com, March 4, 2014, www.space.com/24894-exoplanets-habitable-zone-red-dwarfs.html.

95   there are as many planets as stars: Ethan Siegel, "We Were Wrong: All Stars Don't Have Planets, after All," Big Think, August 10, 2022, https://bigthink.com/starts-with-a-bang/stars-dont-have-planets/.

95   as many as seven Earth-sized planets: Marc Kaufman, "How Many Habitable Zone Planets Can Orbit a Host Star?," NASA, updated November 10, 2022, https://astrobiology.nasa.gov/news/how-many-habitable-zone-planets-can-orbit-a-host-star/.

96   Crocodiles have been roaming: Max Stockdale, "Crocodiles Today Look the Same as They Did 200 Million Years Ago—Our Study Explains Why," *The Conversation*, January 7, 2021, https://theconversation.com/crocodiles-to day-look-the-same-as-they-did-200-million-years-ago-our-study-explains -why-152635.

98   Drake and his associates did plug in: Frank Drake and Dava Sobel, *Is Anyone Out There? The Scientific Search for Extraterrestrial Intelligence* (Delacorte, 1992).

100   Astronomer Stephen Webb: Stephen Webb, "Where Are All the Aliens?" (TED Talk, TED2018, Vancouver, Canada, April 10–14, 2018), www.ted.com /talks/stephen_webb_where_are_all_the_aliens/.

CHAPTER 9

106   In 1959, two Cornell scientists: Giuseppe Cocconi and Philip Morrison, "Searching for Interstellar Communications," *Nature* 184 (September 1959), https://doi.org/10.1038/184844a0.

108   The information in the Electromagnetic Spectrum diagram is from *Ency-clopedia Britannica*, "Electromagnetic Spectrum," updated October 18, 2022, www.britannica.com/science/electromagnetic-spectrum.

109   Project Ozma after the princess of Oz: *Encyclopedia Britannica*, "Project Ozma," updated February 13, 2008, www.britannica.com/event/Project -Ozma.

109   Project Ozma operated from April to July 1960: Seth Shostak, "Project Ozma," SETI Institute, updated July 2021, www.seti.org/project-ozma.

109   approximately 150 hours: *Encyclopedia Britannica*, "Project Ozma."

109   cost only about $2,000: Shostak, "Project Ozma."

109   Tau Ceti and Epsilon Eridani: *Encyclopedia Britannica*, "Project Ozma."

109   the noise came from a passing plane: Frank Drake and Dava Sobel, *Is Anyone Out There? The Scientific Search for Extraterrestrial Intelligence* (Delacorte, 1992), page 38.

110   The James Webb telescope takes pictures: Sarah Braner, "The Colors in the James Webb Space Telescope Photos Are Fake," *Slate*, July 15, 2022, https:// slate.com/technology/2022/07/james-webb-space-telescope-photos-colors -infrared.html.

110   In England in 1967, a young graduate student: Nadia Drake, "Meet the Woman Who Found the Most Useful Stars in the Universe," *National Geographic*, September 6, 2018, www.nationalgeographic.com/science/article/news -jocelyn-bell-burnell-breakthrough-prize-pulsars-astronomy.

112   On August 15, 1977, the Big Ear telescope: Daniela Breitman, "Wow! Signal Explained after 40 Years?," *EarthSky*, June 7, 2017, https://earthsky.org/space /wow-signal-explained-comets-antonio-paris/.

112   Ohio State University: Seth Shostak, "Extraterrestrial Intelligence—Searching for Extraterrestrial Intelligence—SETI—Radio Searches," *Encyclopedia Britannica*, updated December 1, 2021, www.britannica.com/science /extraterrestrial-intelligence/Radio-searches.

112   It lasted seventy-two seconds: Ross Andersen, "The 'Wow!' Signal: One Man's Search for SETI's Most Tantalizing Trace of Alien Life," *The Atlantic*, February 16, 2012, www.theatlantic.com/technology/archive/2012/02/the-wow-signal -one-mans-search-for-setis-most-tantalizing-trace-of-alien-life/253093/.

113   Comet 266P/Christensen: Breitman, "Wow! Signal Explained."

113   One amateur astronomer and YouTuber: Bob Yirka, "Amateur Astronomer Alberto Caballero Finds Possible Source of Wow! Signal," Phys.org, November 24, 2020, https://phys.org/news/2020-11-amateur-astronomer -alberto-caballero-source.html.

114   Earthlings have been using radio waves: Avi Loeb, "When Will We Hear from Extraterrestrials?," *Scientific American*, August 15, 2021, www.scientific american.com/article/when-will-we-hear-from-extraterrestrials/.

114   Radio waves degrade over long distances: Michelle Starr, "Mind-Boggling Image Shows How Far into Space Humanity's Voice Has Actually Reached," ScienceAlert, April 4, 2019, www.sciencealert.com/humanity-hasn-t -reached-as-far-into-space-as-you-think.

114   Also, as Earthly communication improves: Robert Krulwich, "Lucy's Laugh Enlivens the Solar System," NPR, April 21, 2008, www.npr.org/sections /krulwich/2011/08/05/89700174/lucys-laugh-enlivens-the-solar-system.

114   Some radio frequencies are so jammed: Denise Chow, "Humans Are Making It Hard to Listen for Aliens," NBC News, July 2, 2022, www.nbcnews.com /science/ufos-and-aerial-phenomena/humans-are-making-hard-listen-aliens -rcna34752.

114   Green Bank Observatory in West Virginia are "quiet zones": Green Bank Observatory, "National Radio Quiet Zone," accessed October 24, 2022, https:// greenbankobservatory.org/about/national-radio-quiet-zone/.

114   In 2015, Israeli billionaire Yuri Milner: Lee Billings, "Stephen Hawking and Yuri Milner Announce $100M Initiative to Seek ET," *Scientific American*, July 20, 2015, www.scientificamerican.com/article/stephen-hawking-and-yuri -milner-announce-100m-initiative-to-seek-extraterrestrial-intelligence/.

115   A large portion of the money: Daniel Clery, "Listen Up," *Science*, September 10, 2020, www.science.org/content/article/how-big-money-powering -massive-hunt-alien-intelligence.

115   the aim is to listen in on: Breakthrough Initiatives, "Listen," accessed October 24, 2022, https://breakthroughinitiatives.org/initiative/1.

115   Still, Milner has hinted: Clery, "Listen Up."

116   Now SETI scientists can listen: Damond Benningfield, "SETI Gets an Upgrade," *Smithsonian Air & Space*, June 2016, www.smithsonianmag.com /air-space-magazine/new-seti-search-180959126/.

116 One program that's currently operational: George Dvorsky, "New System Would Let Us Know if Aliens Are Using Lasers to Communicate," Gizmodo, December 23, 2021, https://gizmodo.com/new-system-would-let-us-know-if-aliens-are-using-lasers-1848264911.

117 The scientists behind PANOSETI: Robert Sanders, "New Telescope to Look for Laser Pulses from Life around Other Planets," *Berkeley News*, March 2, 2020, https://news.berkeley.edu/story_jump/new-telescope-to-look-for-laser-pulses-from-life-around-other-planets/.

117 quick bursts of light or infrared radiation: Dvorsky, "New System."

117 Prototype telescopes have been installed: Maryanne Campbell, "Innovative Telescopes Set to Detect New Phenomena, Signals from Deep Space," Lick Observatory, February 17, 2021, www.lickobservatory.org/2021/02/17/innovative-telescopes-set-to-detect-new-phenomena-signals-from-deep-space/.

117 Technosignatures: Caleb A. Scharf, "The Origin of Technosignatures," *Scientific American*, July 2, 2021, www.scientificamerican.com/article/the-origin-of-technosignatures/.

118 Dyson estimated that over 3,000 years: Adam Mann, "What Is a Dyson Sphere?," Space.com, August 1, 2019, www.space.com/dyson-sphere.html.

119 Joseph Johann von Littrow suggested: "Human Love for Aliens Clapping One Hand," World Today News, March 23, 2021, www.world-today-news.com/human-love-for-aliens-clapping-one-hand/.

120 Soviets used radio waves to send Morse code: Isobel Whitcomb, "What Messages Have We Sent to Aliens?," *Live Science*, March 20, 2021, www.livescience.com/messages-sent-to-aliens.html.

120 In 1974, Frank Drake, Carl Sagan: Nadia Drake, "40 Years Ago, Earth Beamed Its First Postcard to the Stars," *National Geographic*, November 28, 2014, www.nationalgeographic.com/science/article/40-years-ago-earth-beamed-its-first-postcard-to-the-stars.

120 a stick figure, a diagram of DNA: Arecibo Observatory, "Arecibo Message Project," accessed October 24, 2022, www.naic.edu/challenge/about-message.html.

120 Voyagers 1 and 2, both launched in 1977: National Aeronautics and Space Administration (NASA), "What Are the Contents of the Golden Record?," accessed October 24, 2022, https://voyager.jpl.nasa.gov/golden-record/whats-on-the-record/.

120 The message in Mandarin: NASA, "Greetings to the Universe in 55 Different Languages," accessed October 24, 2022, https://voyager.jpl.nasa.gov/golden-record/whats-on-the-record/greetings/.

120 like in 2018 when a Doritos commercial: Whitcomb, "What Messages."

121 a new METI project called Beacon in the Galaxy: Daniel Oberhaus, "Researchers Made a New Message for Extraterrestrials," *Scientific American*, March 30, 2022, www.scientificamerican.com/article/researchers-made-a-new-message-for-extraterrestrials/.

121 The scientists would like to beam: Kelly Kizer Whitt, "A New Message to the Stars? Beacon in the Galaxy," *EarthSky*, April 21, 2022, https://earthsky.org /space/message-to-the-stars-beacon-in-the-galaxy/.

122 Searching for extraterrestrials takes some coin: Stephen J. Garber, "Searching for Good Science: The Cancellation of NASA's SETI Program," *Journal of the British Interplanetary Society* 52 (1999), https://history.nasa.gov/garber.pdf.

122 created as a nonprofit in 1984: SETI Institute, "History of the SETI Institute," accessed October 24, 2022, www.seti.org/history-seti-institute.

MEET ASTRONOMER JILL TARTER

124 In 1965, she was the only woman: Marina Koren, "Jill Tarter, Feminist Cosmic Icon," *The Atlantic*, July 12, 2017, www.theatlantic.com/science/archive /2017/07/seti-jill-tarter/533322/.

124 she co-founded the nonprofit SETI Institute: SETI Institute, "History of the SETI Institute," accessed October 24, 2022, www.seti.org/history-seti -institute.

124 inspired the character Ellie Arroway: Koren, "Jill Tarter."

124 In 2012, Jill Tarter retired: Mike Wall, "SETI Astronomer Jill Tarter Retiring after 35-Year Alien Hunt," Space.com, May 22, 2012, www.space.com/15801 -jill-tarter-seti-search-retirement.html.

CHAPTER 10

127 The US government has investigated UFOs: Helene Cooper, Ralph Blumenthal, and Leslie Kean, "Glowing Auras and 'Black Money': The Pentagon's Mysterious U.F.O. Program," *New York Times*, December 16, 2017, www .nytimes.com/2017/12/16/us/politics/pentagon-program-ufo-harry-reid.html.

127 three major conclusions: US Air Force, *Unidentified Flying Objects and Air Force Project Blue Book*, USAF Fact Sheet 95-03 (1995), www.nsa.gov/portals /75/documents/news-features/declassified-documents/ufo/usaf_fact_sheet _95_03.pdf.

127 In 2007, the Advanced Aerospace Threat Identification Program: Cooper, Blumenthal, and Kean, "Glowing Auras."

127 San Diego, California: Helene Cooper, Leslie Kean, and Ralph Blumenthal, "2 Navy Airmen and an Object That 'Accelerated like Nothing I've Ever Seen,'" *New York Times*, December 16, 2017, www.nytimes.com/2017/12/16/us /politics/unidentified-flying-object-navy.html.

129 conversations between US Navy crew members: US Department of Defense, "'Look at That Thing': Footage Shows Pilots Spotting Unknown Object," *New York Times*, May 26, 2019, www.nytimes.com/video/us/100000006525294 /ufo-video-navy.html.

130   Office of the Director of National Intelligence: Office of the Director of National Intelligence, *Preliminary Assessment: Unidentified Aerial Phenomena*, June 25, 2021, www.dni.gov/files/ODNI/documents/assessments/Prelimary-Assessment-UAP-20210625.pdf.

133   "Extraordinary claims require extraordinary evidence": Carl Sagan, quoted in Art Harris, "Second View: Sagan on 'Encounters,'" *Washington Post*, December 16, 1977, www.washingtonpost.com/archive/lifestyle/1977/12/16/second-view-sagan-on-encounters/20856d89-a69b-47fa-96d2-202c4a549d8f/.

133   Astronomers in Hawai'i, who were hunting: Dennis Overbye, "Why Oumuamua, the Interstellar Visitor, Looks Eerily Familiar," *New York Times*, updated September 30, 2021, www.nytimes.com/2021/03/23/science/astronomy-oumuamua-comet.html.

133   When the astronomers calculated the trajectory: Mike Wall, "Meet 'Oumuamua, the First-Ever Asteroid from Another Star," *Scientific American*, November 16, 2017, www.scientificamerican.com/article/meet-oumuamua-the-first-ever-asteroid-from-another-star/.

134   Here's what they learned: National Aeronautics and Space Administration (NASA), "'Oumuamua," updated December 19, 2019, https://solarsystem.nasa.gov/asteroids-comets-and-meteors/comets/oumuamua/in-depth/.

135   closest to Earth on October 14: Wall, "Meet 'Oumuamua."

135   by February, it was too distant: Elizabeth Landau, "What We Know—and Don't Know—about 'Oumuamua," NASA, June 27, 2018, https://solarsystem.nasa.gov/news/473/what-we-knowand-dont-knowabout-oumuamua/.

135   Some scientists categorize it as an asteroid: NASA, "'Oumuamua."

135   Avi Loeb, believes 'Oumuamua: Lee Billings, "Astronomer Avi Loeb Says Aliens Have Visited, and He's Not Kidding," *Scientific American*, February 1, 2021, www.scientificamerican.com/article/astronomer-avi-loeb-says-aliens-have-visited-and-hes-not-kidding1/.

136   hundreds of millions of years old: NASA, "'Oumuamua."

137   a fragment of a Pluto-like exoplanet: Theresa Machemer, "New Theory Suggests 'Oumuamua Is a Nitrogen Ice Pancake," *Smithsonian*, March 22, 2021, www.smithsonianmag.com/smart-news/new-theory-suggests-oumuamua-nitrogen-ice-pancake-180977293/.

137   astronomers found their first interstellar comet: NASA, "Comet 2I/Borisov," updated April 20, 2020, https://solarsystem.nasa.gov/asteroids-comets-and-meteors/comets/2I-Borisov/in-depth/.

137   a 2021 report from the Initiative for Interstellar Studies: Matt Williams, "About 7 Interstellar Objects Pass through the Inner Solar System Every Year, Study Estimates," Phys.org, March 15, 2021, https://phys.org/news/2021-03-interstellar-solar-year.html.

CHAPTER 11

139   In June 1947, a rancher: Donovan Webster, "In 1947, a High-Altitude Balloon Crash Landed in Roswell. The Aliens Never Left," *Smithsonian*, July 5, 2017, www.smithsonianmag.com/smithsonian-institution/in-1947-high-altitude -balloon-crash-landed-roswell-aliens-never-left-180963917/.

140   a pilot saw nine UFOs near Mount Rainier: Tony Long, "June 24, 1947: They Came from...Outer Space?," *Wired*, June 24, 2011, www.wired.com/2011/06 /0624first-flying-saucer-sighting/.

140   The wreckage was from Project Mogul: *Encyclopedia Britannica*, "Roswell Incident," updated July 1, 2022, www.britannica.com/event/Roswell-incident.

141   Area 51 is the "top-secret": Alex Ward and Aja Romano, "Area 51 and Aliens: The Myth, the Meme, and the Strange Reality, Explained," *Vox*, September 19, 2019, www.vox.com/2019/9/19/20857221/storm-area-51-aliens-ufos-meme -myth-lore-history-bob-lazar-explained.

142   Nevada Test and Training Range (NTTR): Nellis Air Force Base, "Nevada Test and Training Range," November 2021, www.nellis.af.mil/Units/NTTR/.

142   Before the 1950s, the United States: Ward and Romano, "Area 51 and Aliens."

143   Airline pilots and air traffic controllers: Sebastien Roblin, "The Crazy True Origin Story of Area 51 (and Why People Think UFOs Are There)," *National Interest*, July 20, 2019, https://nationalinterest.org/blog/buzz/crazy-true -origin-story-area-51-and-why-people-think-ufos-are-there-68097.

143   personnel came and went by plane: Ward and Romano, "Area 51 and Aliens."

144   In May 1989, a "witness" named Robert Lazar: Tim McMillan, "Bob Lazar Says the FBI Raided Him to Seize Area 51's Alien Fuel. The Truth Is Weirder," *Vice*, November 13, 2019, www.vice.com/en/article/evjwkw/bob-lazar-says -the-fbi-raided-him-to-seize-area-51s-alien-fuel-the-truth-is-weirder.

144   He claimed to have witnessed alien autopsies: *Encyclopedia Britannica*, "What Is Known (and Not Known) about Area 51," August 14, 2018, www.britannica .com/story/what-is-known-and-not-known-about-area-51.

144   Lazar also bragged to the world: McMillan, "Bob Lazar Says."

145   In the late '90s, Lazar opened a business: Jessica Bennett, "Peddling Poison," *Newsweek*, November 29, 2006, www.newsweek.com/peddling-poison -107327.

145   Lazar had trouble with law enforcement: U.S. Consumer Product Safety Commission, "New Mexico Company Fined, Ordered to Stop Selling Illegal Fireworks Components," news release no. 07-249, July 20, 2007, www.cpsc .gov/Newsroom/News-Releases/2007/New-Mexico-Company-Fined -Ordered-To-Stop-Selling-Illegal-Fireworks-Components.

145   Then, in 2017, while a film crew: McMillan, "Bob Lazar Says."

146   One of the first far-reaching: Shannon Leigh O'Neil, "Close Encounter: When Betty and Barney Hill's Alien Abduction Story Shocked the World," Mental Floss, August 25, 2021, www.mentalfloss.com/article/649683/betty-and-barney-hill-alien-abduction.

148   do not think hypnosis is a reliable way: Johns Hopkins Medicine, "Hypnosis," November 19, 2019, www.hopkinsmedicine.org/health/wellness-and-prevention/hypnosis.

149   Crop Circles, AKA: Alien Street Signs: Rob Irving and Peter Brookesmith, "Crop Circles: The Art of the Hoax," *Smithsonian*, December 15, 2009, www.smithsonianmag.com/arts-culture/crop-circles-the-art-of-the-hoax-2524283/.

149   in 1991 when two Brits claimed: Peter Wilson, "Crop Circles Were Made by Supernatural Forces. Named Doug and Dave," *New York Times*, June 12, 2022, www.nytimes.com/2022/06/12/style/crop-circles.html.

CHAPTER 12

152   The JWST launched on December 25, 2021: "Mission Timeline," Webb Space Telescope, accessed October 24, 2022, https://webbtelescope.org/webb-science/the-observatory/mission-timeline.

152   it will orbit the Sun: National Aeronautics and Space Administration (NASA), "About—Webb Orbit," accessed October 24, 2022, https://webb.nasa.gov/content/about/orbit.html.

152   eighteen lightweight mirrors: NASA, *Webb Space Telescope*, fact sheet, accessed October 24, 2022, www.jwst.nasa.gov/content/webbLaunch/assets/documents/WebbFactSheet.pdf.

152   we will see farther into the universe: "How Does Webb See Back in Time?," Webb Space Telescope, updated May 31, 2018, https://webbtelescope.org/contents/articles/how-does-webb-see-back-in-time.

153   atmosphere of exoplanet WASP-39 b: NASA, "Exoplanet Catalog—WASP-39 b," accessed October 24, 2022, https://exoplanets.nasa.gov/exoplanet-catalog/5673/wasp-39-b/.

153   collaboration between NASA, ESA, CSA; called the Next Generation Space Telescope: NASA, "James Webb Telescope Overview," updated October 20, 2021, www.nasa.gov/mission_pages/webb/about/index.html.

153   The JWST needed a month: Daisy Dobrijevic and Elizabeth Howell, "NASA's James Webb Space Telescope: The Ultimate Guide," Space.com, September 22, 2022, www.space.com/21925-james-webb-space-telescope-jwst.html.

153   it required an additional six months: "Mission & Launch Quick Facts," Webb Space Telescope, accessed October 24, 2022, https://webbtelescope.org/quick-facts/mission-launch-quick-facts.

154   The first sophisticated optical observatory: Christopher Gainor, *Not Yet Imagined: A Study of Hubble Space Telescope Operations* (NASA Office of Communications, 2020), www.nasa.gov/sites/default/files/atoms/files/not_yet_imagined_tagged.pdf.

154   designed to operate for only fifteen years: NASA, "Hubble FAQs," updated October 6, 2022, www.nasa.gov/content/about-facts-hubble-faqs.

154   43.5 feet (13.2 meters) long: NASA, "About the Hubble Space Telescope," updated October 6, 2022, www.nasa.gov/mission_pages/hubble/story/index.html.

154   discovered two of the moons orbiting Pluto: NASA, "Pluto's Two Small Moons Officially Named Nix and Hydra," news release no. 2006-29, June 22, 2006, https://hubblesite.org/contents/news-releases/2006/news-2006-29.html.

154   Hubble helped scientists establish the age: European Space Agency, "Measuring the Age and Size of the Universe," accessed October 24, 2022, https://esahubble.org/science/age_size/.

154   Hubble pictures are all in black and white: Coleman Lowndes, "How Scientists Colorize Photos of Space," *Vox*, updated August 2, 2019, www.vox.com/2019/8/1/20750228/scientists-colorize-photos-space-hubble-telescope.

155   Jupiter and three of its moons: European Space Agency, "JUICE—Science Objectives," updated September 1, 2019, https://sci.esa.int/web/juice/-/50068-science-objectives.

155   Jupiter has quite the magnetosphere: Tatyana Woodall, "Jupiter's Moons Are about to Get JUICE'd for Signs of Life," *Popular Science*, January 6, 2022, www.popsci.com/space/jupiter-moons-juice-mission/.

155   JUICE won't be landing on any moons: NASA, "JUICE," updated January 11, 2019, https://solarsystem.nasa.gov/missions/juice/in-depth/.

155   The journey to Jupiter will take: European Space Agency, "JUICE—Mission Summary," updated September 1, 2019, https://sci.esa.int/web/juice/-/50067-mission-summary.

155   Radar for Icy Moons Exploration (RIME): European Space Agency, "JUICE—Science Payload," updated July 21, 2020, https://sci.esa.int/web/juice/-/50073-science-payload.

155   NASA will head back to the Jovian neighborhood: NASA, "Europa Clipper," accessed October 24, 2022, www.jpl.nasa.gov/missions/europa-clipper.

155   China plans to send an orbiter to Callisto: Andrew Jones, "China Wants to Probe Uranus and Jupiter with 2 Spacecraft on One Rocket," Space.com, September 22, 2022, www.space.com/china-probes-jupiter-uranus-same-launch.

156   this moon is cold (like −290°F, or −179°C): NASA, "Titan—In Depth," updated February 4, 2021, https://solarsystem.nasa.gov/moons/saturn-moons/titan/in-depth/.

156   Dragonfly will land on Titan...take pics: NASA, "Dragonfly Frequently Asked Questions," updated March 17, 2022, www.nasa.gov/dragonfly/frequently-asked-questions/index.html.

156   Dragonfly leaving Earth in 2027…simple life: NASA, "Dragonfly's Journey to Titan," updated March 17, 2022, www.nasa.gov/dragonfly/dragonfly-overview/index.html.

156   The 2000 version gave strong support: Lee Billings, "This Report Could Make or Break the Next 30 Years of U.S. Astronomy," *Scientific American*, August 18, 2021, www.scientificamerican.com/article/this-report-could-make-or-break-the-next-30-years-of-u-s-astronomy/.

156   That program was initiated in 1996: "Mission Timeline," Webb Space Telescope.

157   This headline from *Scientific American*: Lee Billings, "Hunt for Alien Life Tops Next-Gen Wish List for U.S. Astronomy," *Scientific American*, November 4, 2021, www.scientificamerican.com/article/hunt-for-alien-life-tops-next-gen-wish-list-for-u-s-astronomy/.

157   LuvEx is actually the *marriage* of two proposals: Nell Greenfieldboyce, "Astronomers Want NASA to Build a Giant Space Telescope to Peer at Alien Earths," NPR, November 4, 2021, www.npr.org/2021/11/04/1052153703/astronomers-want-nasa-to-build-a-giant-space-telescope-to-peer-at-alien-earths.

157   three times larger than Hubble: Billings, "Hunt for Alien Life."

158   10 billion times fainter than their stars: Chris Wright, "To Study the Next Earth, NASA May Need to Throw Some Shade," *Wired*, January 4, 2022, www.wired.com/story/to-study-the-next-earth-nasa-may-need-to-throw-some-shade/.

158   Like Hubble, LuvEx will detect optical: Billings, "Hunt for Alien Life."

158   sunflower-shaped starshade: Cat Hofacker, "Decadal Survey Wants NASA to Rethink How It Designs Space Telescopes," *Aerospace America*, November 4, 2021, https://aerospaceamerica.aiaa.org/decadal-survey-wants-nasa-to-rethink-how-it-designs-space-telescopes/.

158   estimates an $11 billion…mid-2040s: Billings, "Hunt for Alien Life."

158   Milner's foundation has brought us: Breakthrough Initiatives, "Internet Investor and Science Philanthropist Yuri Milner & Physicist Stephen Hawking Announce Breakthrough Starshot Project to Develop 100 Million Mile per Hour Mission to the Stars within a Generation," accessed October 24, 2022, https://breakthroughinitiatives.org/news/4.

159   The exoplanet Proxima Centauri b: European Southern Observatory, "Planet Found in Habitable Zone around Nearest Star," news release no. eso1629, August 24, 2016, www.eso.org/public/news/eso1629/.

159   The highly reflective lightsails: Ann Finkbeiner, "Inside the Breakthrough Starshot Mission to Alpha Centauri," *Scientific American*, December 22, 2016, www.scientificamerican.com/article/inside-the-breakthrough-starshot-mission-to-alpha-centauri/.

159   Each StarChip will also weigh: Breakthrough Initiatives, "Concept," accessed October 24, 2022, https://breakthroughinitiatives.org/concept/3.

159   the size of a postage stamp: Karl Tate, "How Breakthrough Starshot's Interstellar Probes Would Work (Infographic)," Space.com, April 12, 2016, www.space.com/32551-breakthrough-starshot-interstellar-spacecraft-infographic.html.

159   they'll be packed…reach their destination: Breakthrough Initiatives, "Internet Investor."

160   This is simply a flyby: Finkbeiner, "Inside the Breakthrough Starshot."

160   even space dust could destroy them: Ethan Siegel, "Ask Ethan: Could the 'Breakthrough Starshot' Project Even Survive Its Planned Journey?," Big Think, January 7, 2022, https://bigthink.com/starts-with-a-bang/breakthrough-starshot-survive/.

160   send up lots and lots…thousands of them: Finkbeiner, "Inside the Breakthrough Starshot."

161   Our closest star system is the Alpha Centauri system: *Encyclopedia Britannica*, "Alpha Centauri," updated May 23, 2022, www.britannica.com/place/Alpha-Centauri.

162   Ever since Chuck Yeager "broke" the sound barrier: *Encyclopedia Britannica*, "Chuck Yeager," updated September 16, 2022, www.britannica.com/biography/Chuck-Yeager.

162   Einstein's theory of special relativity: *Encyclopedia Britannica*, "Special Relativity," updated September 7, 2022, www.britannica.com/science/special-relativity.

163   That's fast enough to circle Earth: Melissa Petruzzello, "Will Light-Speed Space Travel Ever Be Possible?," *Encyclopedia Britannica*, July 19, 2019, www.britannica.com/story/will-light-speed-space-travel-ever-be-possible.

163   These hypothetical bridges: Nola Taylor Tillman and Ailsa Harvey, "What Is Wormhole Theory?," Space.com, January 13, 2022, www.space.com/20881-wormholes.html.

165   it took Perseverance about seven months: NASA, "Mission Timeline—Cruise," accessed October 24, 2022, https://mars.nasa.gov/mars2020/timeline/cruise/.

165   Estimates say we could reach Mars: Fraser Cain, "Earth to Mars in 100 Days: The Power of Nuclear Rockets," Phys.org, July 1, 2019, https://phys.org/news/2019-07-earth-mars-days-power-nuclear.html.

165   one company's goal is for the journey: Chris Young, "A 123,000 MPH Nuclear Rocket Could Reach Mars in Only One Month," Interesting Engineering, September 21, 2021, https://interestingengineering.com/science/a-123000-mph-nuclear-rocket-could-reach-mars-in-only-one-month.

165   in 2019, the US government approved $125 million: Jeff Foust, "Momentum Grows for Nuclear Thermal Propulsion," *SpaceNews*, May 22, 2019, https://spacenews.com/momentum-grows-for-nuclear-thermal-propulsion/.

166   Earth's temperature will rise: Bob Berman, *Earth-Shattering: Violent Super-novas, Galactic Explosions, Biological Mayhem, Nuclear Meltdowns, and Other Hazards to Life in Our Universe* (Little, Brown, 2019), page 279.

168   the SETI community does have some guidelines: SETI Institute, "Protocols for an ETI Signal Detection," April 23, 2018, www.seti.org/protocols-eti -signal-detection.

INDEX

Page numbers in *italics* refer to illustrations in the text.

Cora McAnulty

STACY McANULTY

is an award-winning children's book author and former mechanical engineer (and before that—like, in fourth grade—an aspiring astronaut). Her love of math and science is reflected in most of her books. She writes chapter books; middle-grade novels, including *The Miscalculations of Lightning Girl*; middle-grade nonfiction, including *Save the People! Halting Human Extinction*; and picture books, including the Our Universe series, which explores space and the natural world. She has not seen a UAP or received a message from deep space—*yet*! Originally from New York, she now lives in North Carolina with her family. Stacy invites you to visit her online at stacymcanulty.com.